'This is a very timely, wide-rangi[ng]
of a subject that needs to be tak[en]
well.'
Rev Dr Russ Parker, author of Hea[ling]
of 2Restore; Healing Church Wounds

'Peter's costly experience in the deliverance ministry, combined
with his scriptural knowledge and understanding, make this a
book full of wise and practical guidance. *Light and Liberty* is a
thought-provoking read, offering perceptive insights. It is the
fruit of the author's own loving service and faithful witness in
the community.'
Mark Rylands, Bishop of Shrewsbury

'In *Light and Liberty*, Peter Mockford draws upon his wide-
ranging experience as a parish priest, leader of a diocesan
deliverance team and a practising psychotherapist to present a
comprehensive portrayal of healing and deliverance. Peter
stresses the vital importance of understanding and practising
deliverance in the Church today, since it was so central to
Christ's thinking, teaching and practice. In the book Peter
addresses many relevant issues surrounding deliverance –
discernment, power, relationships, idolatry, curses and the
occult – in a way that is well researched and well written. He
refers extensively to recent books, as well as to the biblical text.
Light and Liberty is a clear and definitive call to action for the
Church of England – and the wider Christian Church. It is
destined to be widely read, often referred to and repeatedly put
into practice in the coming days. *Light and Liberty* is a gift from
God for the Church at this time.'
*Robert Mountford, County Ecumenical Mission Officer for
Staffordshire and the Black Country*

'The ministry of deliverance will often be seen as controversial
and divisive, and, as such, will be conveniently ignored by many.

Congratulations to my good friend and colleague, Peter Mockford, for not shying away from this difficult subject but choosing to tackle it head on. Having led a diocesan deliverance team for many years and also being a qualified, so-called, "secular" psychotherapist, he is more qualified than most to balance the fine line between deliverance, psychiatry and psychotherapy. This is a book rooted in biblical truth but also in years of experience at the coalface of seeking to help those in need and to answer the prayer that pleads "deliver us from evil".'

Lloyd Cooke, Chief Executive, Saltbox Christian Centre

'Evil is a reality, and those who have examined and experienced the claims of the Christian faith are fully aware of the destructive power and influence of evil entities. Rev Trevor Dearing made national news in the early 1970s with his deliverance ministry at St Paul's church in Hainault, Essex, when thousands were queuing to get into his small church over a period of a few months. I was very blessed to have spent much time with Trevor and Anne Dearing in the early 1980s and learnt how important this ministry was and how misunderstood it was, even in the Evangelical, Pentecostal and Charismatic Community (EPC). From this perspective, I have found Peter's book a ground-breaking, encouraging, positive and necessary contribution to this much-needed teaching within the Christian community. When public theology and social science engage in these eternal realities then many will find true freedom.

'I believe there is a shift starting to take place in the public space that may start to see some reverses from the impact of some of the negative aspects of the Enlightenment. Faith and Reason can co-exist. This is a re-engagement within the public space from a faith perspective which hopefully will move faith from being "private" to being "personal". This may well open the doors again for a discussion about cultural and spiritual capital which will encourage the Christian community to re-engage through her mandate of love and freedom in Christ. The deliverance ministry will be at the forefront of this re-engagement and awakening. It will require great godly wisdom and discernment from a motivation of genuine godly love in Christ. Peter's excellent book knocks at this door with authority and a heavenly mandate: a biblically based understanding of the book of Acts and authentic discipleship with the true love of Jesus Christ as the foundation of this much-needed Jesus-based ministry.

'*Light and Liberty* is a book for our times and essential reading for those who are serious about their Christian commitment and love of others. Peter is a practical theologian and academic and a great blessing to the body of Christ.'
Chris Cole, Founder of Cross Rhythms Radio

'This is an important book since there is a big lack of balance on this subject. We either never talk about it, or become scared, or try to find patterns to pray in every detail and lose track of the big picture. As both vicar and psychotherapist, Peter Mockford has overview and wisdom, and long experience in working with deliverance issues. He points out the most important: that it is all a question of a relationship with the Lord, where we listen and try, getting it wrong sometimes, but hopefully getting it right more and more often, as we do it together. As Peter points out, this ministry of deliverance, in its widest sense, is at the core of Jesus' ministry. As followers of Jesus, it should be at ours too.'
Birgitta Sjöström Aasa, pastor, Church of Sweden, and consultant in Sweden for the international inter-church prayer ministry VMTC: Victorious Ministry through Christ (Helhet genom Kristus)

'Peter Mockford's book is extremely challenging for the contemporary western European models of rational thoughts. In the well-known survey "Changing Mass Priorities: The Link Between Modernization and Democracy" (2010), the authors Ronald Inglehart and Christian Welzel present a global cultural map of 53 societies by two value-scales: survival vs self-expression values, and traditional vs secular-rational values. Not surprisingly, Sweden is world-leading in secular-rational self-expression values. Other western European societies, like Britain, are not far behind. It is likely, I dare to say obvious, that the churches in our countries have been strongly affected by these values. Sometimes it is a result of a lack of a deep Christian, biblical identity; sometimes because the Church, for evangelistic reasons, adapts to this like Paul at the Aeropagus, in order to reach "modern thinking" people with the gospel.

'Peter's book, describing the spiritual realm and how to deal with such issues, drops like a bomb into our rational thinking world. Peter is literal in his biblical approach and embraces many traditional values. He balances issues about psychology, psychiatry, psychotherapy and deliverance in an admirable and honest way.

'This book gives us essential tools and increased insight in the matter of deliverance ministry. Let us be challenged! Let us test everything, and hold fast to what is good (1 Thessalonians 5:21).'
Magnus Aasa, vicar in the Evangelical-Lutheran Swedish Church, parish of Halmstad

LIGHT AND LIBERTY

REDISCOVERING THE POWER
OF DELIVERANCE

Peter Mockford

**instant
apostle**

First published in Great Britain in 2017

Instant Apostle
The Barn
1 Watford House Lane
Watford
Herts
WD17 1BJ

British Library Cataloguing-in-Publication Data

A catalogue record for this book is available from the British Library

This book and all other Instant Apostle books are available from Instant Apostle:

Website: www.instantapostle.com

E-mail: info@instantapostle.com

ISBN 978-1-909728-63-9

Printed in Great Britain

This book is dedicated to the loving and supporting family of the Church of Dresden and Blurton. Particular thanks to Theo and Linda.

Author's note

Identifying characteristics have been changed to protect identities.

Contents

Foreword

As I write, the Christian Church is celebrating that time of the liturgical year when it remembers All Saints.

The Saints are men and women of this and every age who have lived out their faith in Jesus Christ through their daily lives. Some have made dramatic sacrifices but others have simply been true to the teachings of the gospel and reflected the love of Christ to those around them. They have all been like bright lights shining in a world so often full of darkness, illuminating a better way and pointing people to God.

But we cannot forget that the Eve of All Saints Day is 31 October, and that this 'Hallowe'en' has become synonymous with the very darkness that the Light of Christ dispels. Hallowe'en is now big business with all kinds of decorations and costumes and 'special' food aimed at the many who have parties to celebrate this annual journey into the macabre. Leaving aside the genuine fear of some who become subjected to 'trick or treat', the willingness of parents to introduce their children to tales of witches and ghosts and rattling bones is a marked contrast to their reluctance to tell them the good news of Jesus Christ!

Of course, this scenario is a far cry from satanic ritual abuse, psychological trauma or other manifestations of evil that are confronted by deliverance ministry, but Hallowe'en often serves as a kind of 'introduction' to the occult and other dangerous forms of spirituality that pervade our twenty-first century society at a time when more 'traditional' forms of institutionalised religion appear to be losing their popularity.

It is therefore very timely that Peter Mockford has produced this clear, practical and immensely helpful reflection on deliverance ministry today. Although primarily for those involved with this ministry, Peter writes in a way that is accessible for any interested in this key part of the teaching of Jesus – which I believe should be all who try to follow Christ. As Peter indicates, 'Christ challenged evil whenever he met it' because evil destroys our relationship with God.

Peter has served in an exciting but demanding parish in Stoke-on-Trent since 1994 and has played a key part in the deliverance ministry of Lichfield Diocese since 1995. In 2004 he was awarded a distinction in MSc in Integrative Psychotherapy and has served as a member of the Diocesan Counselling Team since that time. He is highly regarded by his colleagues and was invited to become a Prebendary of Lichfield Cathedral in recognition of his ministry. Everything he does is rooted in daily prayer and Bible study and evolves from a strong sense of pastoral care and commitment.

It is an honour to be associated with this valuable contribution to our thinking about the deliverance ministry.

Bishop Geoffrey Stafford
All Saints Day, 2016

Introduction

In 2016 we have seen some of the greatest changes in my lifetime take place in the Western world's political climate. The UK voted for Brexit, and the USA voted for Donald Trump. Across Europe there are stirrings for the anti-establishment political parties. This is coupled with a huge rise in refugees, from Africa, and the war zones in the Middle East.

We are, I suspect, in for a time of massive social change in the West over the coming years; in part this will be because the political systems cannot deliver all the changes they have promised. In this environment fear can easily rise, and along with fear, anger. When this happens the hidden fault lines of society get flushed to the surface. In the wake of the Brexit vote for example there was a rise in racial crimes. Within my own church, those of different ethnic roots were abused and threatened.

As old securities are shown to be empty, the Church has a great opportunity to share the love and message of Jesus. However along with the fears and anger coming to the surface so will the demonic. The Church in the widest sense has to be equipped to be 'the good news'; critical to this is the ministry of deliverance, literally setting the captives free.

This book was written for the local church. Each church of whatever denomination, is charged with bringing in the kingdom of God, not with our power, but with His. We have to take the calling and responsibility seriously. I pray that this book will help and equip you and your church in this vital ministry. Please do use the web site resources at www.restoring-the-apple.org. At this website you will find a six-session course on equipping your church in this ministry. This course was developed in the local church, and from it came this book.

May God bless you, and surround you with His love and protection.

Peter Mockford
November 2016

Chapter 1
The Context of the Deliverance Ministry

In October 1993 John Widdas and I published the book, *Lightning from Heaven*.[1] This was a reflection on our experiences in St Editha's, Tamworth, in the previous four years. We were looking particularly at the whole area of spiritual warfare and the demonic. Since then John has gone to glory, and time has moved on. I have been the vicar of Blurton and Dresden for the last 20 years, and have led the Lichfield Anglican diocesan deliverance team for the last eight years.

It has been a time of huge changes in society and not least in the Church. In the late 1980s and early nineties there was a lot of publicity surrounding satanic ritual abuse, with cases hitting the headlines on a regular basis. In 1991 Andrew Boyd published his investigation into this area, *Blasphemous Rumours*.[2] His reports of the survivors of abuse are as harrowing to read now as they were then. The abuse has not gone away, but now there are specialised psychotherapeutic agencies that deal with the psychological trauma. This is led in the United Kingdom

---

[1] Kingsway, 1993.

[2] Andrew Boyd, *Blasphemous Rumours* (London: Fount, 1991).

particularly by the Trauma Abuse Group, who through their website can point survivors to the necessary agencies for help.[3] Satanic ritual abuse has not gone away.

Today there is a huge emphasis on being fulfilled as an individual, doing the things that build me up, having a successful life. This in itself is neither new nor bad, but its main expression has been the incredible rise of consumerism. This is in turn partly fed by the increasing advances in technology, so it becomes important to have the latest phone, and the latest gadget, because if I have these, according to advertising, then my life will be better. Technology, we are told, can meet our basic needs, so contact with others comes more and more through social media, and less face-to-face. However, there is, I believe, a backlash setting in. This was beautifully illustrated by a recent advert in the UK for a broadband provider. The customer is getting poor service on her broadband and gets so frustrated that she throws away her computer and goes to live in a wood, carving wooden spoons. Getting back to basics, getting back to some kind of spirituality that gives me fulfilment is becoming more important. To fill this need there is now a vast area of different kinds of spiritualities; these promise all sorts of benefits. It is perhaps surprising that the Church has not seen an upsurge in numbers as a result of this. There have been developments in the monastic movements, and Celtic spirituality, to mention two; however, overall church attendance, particularly in the Church of England, is static. Part of the reason for this must be that in a society dominated by rules and laws, the

---

[3] http://www.tag-uk.net (accessed 31st October 2016).

perception of the Church is similar, and what people do not want in Western society is more rules. Indeed, it is the 'fresh expressions of Church', which are perceived to be different, that have seen the most growth. The attraction of alternative spiritualities, which are exotic, different, deal with the body (and have rules, but unfamiliar ones), is easy to see.

John Pritchard, in his book, *The Life and Work of a Priest* puts it this way:

> Spirituality is clearly very popular today. It usually seems to have a somewhat Eastern flavour and is associated with wisdom, experience, mysticism and self-help. Spirituality is contrasted favourably with religion in a clear stand-off. Spirituality is seen to be about freedom, and religion about control; spirituality is open, and religion is narrow-minded; spirituality is accepting, and religion is judgemental. The priest has to understand the depth of this dichotomy in order to face it seriously, while also recognizing that people's fascination with spirituality may be a hunger for the holy which Christian faith is well able to address if offered sensitively and intelligently.[4]

There is another factor that is rapidly approaching Western society, and that is the rise of automation. Listening to a BBC Radio 4 programme in February 2016 on this issue, the point was made that for the last 30 years,

---

[4] John Pritchard, *The Life and Work of a Priest* (London: SPCK 2007) p.45.

identity has been closely associated with work. I am what I do. As this diminishes in the next 50 years or so, the search for identity will in part be I am what I believe. This offers great opportunities for the Christian faith, as John Pritchard points out.

This ever-changing river of spirituality, in which the gospel is shared, has a lot in common with the context of the early Church. However, unlike the early Church, we have in the main lost one of the key gifts and ministries that Jesus had and shared with His followers: the ministry of deliverance, dealing with evil. This book is about getting back this key ministry into the life of the Church.

Current state of the deliverance ministry

Within society there is, thanks to modern technology, instant access to news, and nothing remains private for very long. If you want to know something now, you google it! This has had profound consequences for the Church. Historical abuses can no longer be covered up; there is now little or no security in trusting the old boys' network to keep things out of the public eye. On the whole, this has been a good thing. But for those involved in the deliverance ministry, this means a major rethink on how we do things and how open we are. Traditionally, the Church as a whole has always kept this ministry quiet, as something that is necessary but not very savoury! You have to have it, but it does not taste very nice!

If something is hidden or put away, it begs the question, why? There is always the potential that it is something that is either dangerous or fearful and should not be touched, or it is something that is shameful, and therefore needs to hidden away. I suspect that both have affected the Church's deliverance ministry. The origins of the shame that surround this ministry lie in part in our history. We are all, in Western society, products of the Enlightenment. That was a period in history in the seventeenth and eighteenth centuries where there was a rediscovery of reason and individualism. This was in contrast to the accepted wisdom and supremacy of the Church.

It is not particularly rational to believe in evil as involving, in part, real demons. But is it any more rational to believe in a physical resurrection from the dead? There is perhaps a more honest reason as to why the deliverance ministry is kept hidden, and that is to do with our make-up as human beings. All of us have things and parts of us that we are ashamed of. However, because we don't like looking at these things, we project our sense of unease and shame into other places. This enables us to acknowledge our emotions at arm's length; it doesn't enable us to process our emotions, but we have to put them somewhere. If there was any area in Christian ministry that causes unease it is this area, so it is a good place to put those emotions. This is called projection. Projection is putting those emotions we do not want to own onto another area. This applies equally to institutions like the Church as well as to individuals.

Likewise, with fear, this area of ministry can play into our deep subconscious fears of the unknown, the deadly, the fear of death. The trouble is that it is all too easy to place this fear onto the deliverance ministry, and not to deal with the issues in ourselves.

Now, there is truth in the fact that the deliverance ministry is rarely pleasant, and it always involves dealing with hurt, sometimes very confused, people, but it was a component part of the ministry of Jesus, and He was always upfront about it. Today I believe we have to be upfront with this ministry as it has a critical role to play in the life and mission of Church in the widest sense. However, part of being upfront will involve dealing with our projections onto the ministry. This will not be straightforward nor easy, but as Jesus put it:

> The Spirit of the Lord is on me,
> because he has anointed me
> to proclaim good news to the poor.
> He has sent me to proclaim freedom for the
> prisoners
> and recovery of sight for the blind,
> to set the oppressed free.
> *Luke 4:18*

We all need that freedom. So to minister in this area means being prepared to face one's own fears, and grow in wholeness.

Psychology

For some, both within and outside the Church, there is extreme scepticism about this ministry. This can have what seem to be valid roots in the body of knowledge encompassed by psychology, psychiatry and psychotherapy. Fifteen years ago similar questions were arising in my mind, and I felt that it was right to train as a secular psychotherapist. The four years of training were perhaps the most challenging, painful, exhilarating and healing time I have ever experienced. They were also deeply searching, as I was forced to integrate my theology with what I was learning. This is an ongoing process!

Psychotherapy has its roots at the beginning of the twentieth century, with Freud, Jung and others. In the later part of the century we have Fritz Perls and Carl Rogers, to mention just two. In the main it is the attempt to understand and articulate the nature of being human. The evidence base is predominantly observational and experiential, but more recently it is getting closely connected with neurobiology. Of particular importance is how we as humans develop and relate. It is generally agreed that the key factor in our development is our relationships from our very earliest days, and that this, along with our genetic make-up, determines how we relate and our mental health as adults.

Interestingly, a number of the key figures in psychotherapy came from either a Jewish or Christian background. In the main they rejected their faith history, but in their thinking and writing this still came through. Indeed, if you read Carl Rogers' (the founder of person-centred therapy) core conditions they could have come from the teachings of Christ! Psychotherapy, though, was not restricted to understanding; the aim was to bring healing, and enable people to live lives that were fulfilled. The identified key component of being fulfilled was the ability to form healthy relationships.

Not surprisingly there was historically considerable antagonism between faith and psychotherapy.

Psychotherapy saw faith as a way of avoiding looking at oneself, and faith constructs simply as a way of projecting out what was inside. For example, God as a judge was simply the projection of the pain felt and experienced at the hands of a judgemental father.

Psychotherapy saw the way forward as looking at and dealing with what was inside, not looking outside to an external source for help. Faith, on the other hand, saw psychotherapy as denying the existence of God, being human-centred in its essence, and saying in effect that faith was invalid and toxic.

In recent years, though, these positions have mellowed. Psychotherapy has recognised (in the main) that spirituality and faith plays an important part in the well-being of being human. Most of the main Christian denominations in the UK now recognise the validity and need for psychotherapy/counselling, and send those in need to appropriately qualified persons.

Both the Christian faith and psychotherapy hold in common the primacy of relationships. For the Christian the primary relationship is with Christ; for the psychotherapist it is between client and therapist. Any relationship always involves both the other and myself, so what is needed is reaching to the other, recognising the relational dynamics, and recognising my own internal dynamics. This is held in common with both faith and psychotherapy. Both faith and psychotherapy have the potential to inform the other, albeit coming from different starting points.

This has particular relevance to the deliverance ministry, as it is very easy to blame demons for something which is in reality an issue for oneself. Psychotherapists have long warned against using a faith structure to avoid personal issues. However, because psychotherapy deals in relational dynamics it can inform faith dynamics, which at their core are relational with God and with my fellow human beings. The opposite is also true as faith encompasses being aware of what is beyond oneself, and allows for a greater vision of engagement with the source of love, God Himself.

When we look at understanding any issue, and in this case the deliverance ministry, we do so through the filters that we have in our minds. These filters are a result of culture, education and upbringing. But for the Christian and, interestingly, for the psychotherapist, the primary filter needs to be relational. The whole reason that Jesus came was to restore our relationship with the Father, and with each other.

Going forward

The deliverance ministry draws its remit from the Lord's Prayer '… but deliver us from the evil one [or evil]' (see Matthew 6:9-13). To be delivered from something is to be set free from it so it no longer influences or controls you. Freedom is to be no longer bound by the present, past, or demonic to reach the potential that God has for you and me; that is real deliverance. Paul puts it this way: 'It is for freedom that Christ has set us free' (Galatians 5:1). For the Christian, freedom is living in the empowering, life-giving relationship with Christ, which is why 'deliver us from … evil' (Matthew 6:13) is said in the relational context of the Lord's Prayer. This is not normally how we think about freedom; we use the word to mean that restrictions have been done away with, that we are free from prison, or free from debt. Freedom for the Christian is relational; freedom is to be in relationship with God.

If Christ came to bring freedom, then the deliverance ministry plays a key role in mission. The Mark version of the Great Commission includes, 'And these signs will accompany those who believe: in my name they will drive out demons; they will speak in new tongues' (Mark 16:17). Now, even given the fact that this may be a later addition to the Gospel, the activity in Acts with demons lends credence to the fact that it was a component part of the early Christian message of good news.

Today there is little doubt that people are getting exposed to a much wider variety of spiritual practices, and are searching for a spirituality that is meaningful to them. Some of these are without a doubt not good for your health, such as Ouija boards, etc. Perhaps less blatant than occultic activities but equally hazardous are types of meditative techniques that can also be less than spiritually neutral.

So this means that the vast majority of people have a range of spiritual experience, to which the Church needs to be relevant. It is not enough for the Church to embrace all in a quasi-niceness; we have to be able to speak and act with the love of Christ. That means getting rid of the demonic when needed. This is part of our identity as children of God, that evil will be challenged and not allowed to act. This may sound a bit dramatic and dogmatic, but Jesus was quite clear about His boundaries and what He regarded as acceptable and unacceptable. Evil in all its forms was unacceptable. Christ challenged evil where He met it, whether this was demonic, or within the practices of the religious institutions of the day. This made Him hugely popular with the ordinary person on the street, who was oppressed in the name of God, but did not win Him friends and popularity contests with the religious leaders of the day. However, this is not a charter for dogmatic authority, because Jesus drew His authority and discernment from the living relationship with the Father, not from a book of rules. Jesus had a heart of compassion that put people first above laws; what He did was motivated by love, not by law. He welcomed the outcast – just look at His disciples! He touched the leper, and loved the unloved.

Evil was challenged by Christ because it destroys our relationship with God. For Jesus, a component part of dealing with evil was the deliverance ministry. It is as relevant now as it was in Jesus' day, and it is for the Church now. The deliverance ministry is part of bringing the love of God to this society; it may well not sit comfortably, but Jesus did not do comfort!

Terminology

When talking about this area, the terminology can get confusing and overlap. So to attempt some form of clarity, this is what I mean when talking about:

- Demonic and satanic: this refers to demons and the person of Satan.

- Evil: this refers to the characteristic of the demonic, human beings and nature, where harm is wished upon the relationship with God and each other.

- Sin: this is the act that damages the relationship with God and each other.

- Healing: the restoration of wholeness in whatever form: physical, psychological or spiritual.

- Deliverance: the getting rid of the demonic and its influence.

- Exorcism: a very specific term applied to getting rid of a demonic spirit that has overwhelmed a human personality. This is a rare occurrence.

- Oppression: this is the effect of demons, humans, society, where it is negative and working against the life-giving relationship with God.

- Curses: the deliberate wishing of evil on another.

Chapter 2
Understanding of the Deliverance Ministry

At one level, it is extremely difficult to know where the deliverance ministry begins and ends. If the remit is from the Lord's Prayer and the ministry of Jesus, then clearly it is focused around the dealing with the demonic. But it does not stop there; the Lord's Prayer clearly sees deliverance as dealing with evil in the widest sense. There is no reference in the Lord's Prayer, for example, to healing, because presumably it falls under the category of evil. So drawing clear lines of demarcation is not easy, or perhaps even desirable. Perhaps the best one can do is to say the focus is clearest with the demonic, but that does not preclude dealing with evil in all its shapes and forms, and that will always involve healing. For example, if someone has deliberately involved themselves in the occult, then there is a high likelihood that there will be a demonic presence that has to be dealt with, but why they involved themselves could well relate to emotional wounds that need healing.

Understanding always informs how you deal with something, so understanding the nature of good and evil is important. In Genesis 1 there is the great comment of

God: 'God saw all that he had made, and it was very good' (Genesis 1:31). In creation there was something at the very beginning that was of God and was good, because it came from God. Unfortunately, there then came the business of the fruit. The temptation of the serpent was to challenge what God had said, and somehow make out that God was being self-serving (Genesis 3:1-5). Eve was quite clear about what God had said (Genesis 3:3) so she knew that she was doing wrong. She and Adam knew what the boundaries of the relationship were with God, and broke them. No longer was God going to be the point of reference in their lives, but they were going to be their own point of reference. They were the ones who would now decide what was good and what was evil.

However, there was a very high price for this decision. Firstly, we are told that shame came into the world: 'they realised they were naked ... they hid from the Lord God' (Genesis 3:7-8). The relationship with God was no longer free from guilt and shame. A fundamental shift had taken place; the relationship could never again be the same. In the rest of Genesis chapter 3, we read of the consequences of eating the fruit.

There is an irrevocable shift in the relationship between humankind and God. The picture of the Garden of Eden is one of openness, of being at ease with both oneself and with God, of harmony with nature and with one another. There is also an honouring of the relationship with God; there is a dependency and recognition that He determines good and evil. All of this changes with the serpent and the fruit. There is genuine choice, though: both Eve and Adam choose to eat. In doing so, they place themselves at the centre. They will determine what is good and what is evil; no longer will the relationship with God determine what is right and wrong. As the serpent puts it, 'you will be like God' (Genesis 3:5). This is, to use classical terms, the sin of idolatry. Relationally, our point of reference is now ourselves, not our relationship with God.

At the very beginning we were created to be in relationship with God. We were created by the breath of God (Genesis 2:7); life was to be lived in relationship with Him. This went by the board very quickly. But God is incredibly loving, and indeed defined by love (1 John 4:8). That incredible verse, 'For God so loved the world that he gave his one and only Son' (John 3:16), has to a degree lost its impact with its overuse. But the fact is that God took the initiative to fix the relationship, and He did so by giving (which implies letting go), with no strings attached, His only Son. This is unconditional love. God did not say, 'Well, if the world repents, I will send My Son.' No, God sent Him; this is love given without conditions.

It should come as no surprise that in the first three Gospels the public ministry of Jesus begins with His baptism, which is then followed by the temptations in the desert. There is the echo here of the Garden of Eden. If Jesus falls to the temptations of power, wealth and idolatry, His ministry is totally compromised, because His relationship to His Father fundamentally changes. But unlike Adam and Eve in the Garden of Eden, He holds to His calling and relationship with the Father. Paul recognised this dynamic:

> But Christ has indeed been raised from the dead,
> the firstfruits of those who have fallen asleep. For

since death came through a man, the resurrection
of the dead comes also through a man. For as in
Adam all die, so in Christ all will be made alive.
1 Corinthians 15:20-22

Sins, then, are those things that destroy and detract from relationships, particularly the relationship with God. The focal point of sin is idolatry, as this places the point of reference of living away from the relationship with God.

Sin in the Garden of Eden was a choice. But sometimes sin is not a choice, it is a function of history and upbringing. No human being has had perfect parenting, so for all of us there are inbuilt aspects of our personality that work against relationships. These we did not deliberately put in place, but developed in the main to survive. However, because they are adaptations we make when very young, they rarely serve us well relationally when we are older. For example, a child may well have learned to be very quiet when young as otherwise they got hit. In later life, though, this mechanism does not work well relationally, as keeping quiet and not engaging with others does not build relationships. This is sin in that it works against relationships – it is certainly not the fault of the individual, but they will have to deal with it at some point to develop relationships. Sometimes the effects of our early upbringing are devastating.

Jenny was adopted at about four months old. She was of mixed race, never knew her father, and only in later years her birth mother. But she was abandoned at birth in a house and only rescued on the fourth day. Despite being adopted, the terror of abandonment and the need to be rescued never left her. The internal pain resulted in alcohol and drug abuse in later life. To her deep credit she had the courage to face and work these issues through, but her original experience had profound sinful effects in later life. It was never her fault, but she bore the consequences of sin that were then passed down a generation.

This was recognised by the Church and enshrined in the doctrine of original sin. This says that because of the sin of Adam, there is something innate in human beings that means they are sinful. However, this is controversial and hard to accept – how can a newborn baby be sinful? This is perhaps because we have linked sin to personal guilt, but in the in the majority of cases sin is not linked to personal guilt. However, the doctrine does point to an important truth: there is something deeply rooted about sin that can go from generation to generation.

In the Old Testament, the consequences of sin were deeply profound for the individual and also for the community. This then affected subsequent generations. For example, Abraham, Isaac and Ishmael. Here Hagar, the Egyptian servant of Abraham, bore him a son, Ishmael, but it was not the son of his wife, Sarah. The son Sarah bore, Isaac, was the son that God promised – Isaac was son of the promise, not Ishmael. The result was that Ishmael and Hagar were sent away by Abraham to die in the desert, but God rescued them. Ishmael is seen as the forerunner of the Arab nations and Isaac the beginning of the Israelites. Between the two there is trouble (Genesis 16:11-12). This has gone down the generations to the present day.

There is growing evidence that environmental factors can have an effect on DNA, which can subsequently affect future generations. This impacts on the future generations' behaviour. In effect, sin is being passed down even in our DNA.[5]

Sin is all that negatively affects our relationships, firstly with God and then with each other. It is the primary aim of the devil to cause sin, as sin separates and compromises our relationships. We have to separate out, though, sin from guilt – it is not my fault how my parents treated me. But it is my responsibility to own who I am and deal with it. It is my responsibility to see that God came to bring life in its fullness. 'The thief comes only to steal and kill and destroy; I have come that they may have life, and have it to the full' (John 10:10). Jesus came to bring us life in its fullness, deliverance in all its facets, freedom from the demonic, healings from the wounds of sin, so that the relationships I form firstly with God and then with others are life-giving.

So when God is dealing with Israel it is no surprise that the commandments are relational throughout. In fact, the first four commandments are directly related to our relationship with God (Exodus 20:3-8; Deuteronomy 5:6-12). In summary they read as: no other gods before Me, and no idols; do not misuse the name of the Lord; keep the Sabbath. So a biblical view of good and evil is directly related to the relationship we have firstly with God and secondly with each other. So what promotes the relationship with God is good and what detracts is evil. This is not just personal but involves communities and nations.

---

[5] https://www.newscientist.com/article/dn27658-first-evidence-of-how-parents-lives-could-change-childrens-dna/ (accessed 31st October 2016).

If we are created as the world, as communities, as individuals to receive life by being in relationship with God, but choose not to, then the result, as Paul puts it very graphically, is death: 'For the wages of sin is death' (Romans 6:23). Interestingly, the word that Paul uses for wages is the word that was used for a soldier's pay. We talk about serving in the army, so payment is for who you serve; or in other words, who you are in relationship with, and to whom you have given your allegiance. Paul is saying that if you choose to sin or choose not to deal with sin that has been done to you, then you will pay the price. Because sin operates in our relationship with God and each other, choosing not to deal with it means that we are choosing ourselves over and above our relationship with God and others. This cuts us off from the source of life which is the relationship with God. It is this failure that means death, not perhaps literally now, but certainly relationally and spiritually.

Sin is by definition evil, as it works against that which is life-giving. But evil is not just seen in terms of the demonic, although it is here that it has its tightest focus; we see it in terms of what human beings do to each other, and we see it in nature.

It is perhaps one of the most disturbing findings of modern psychological research that the effects of relationships, positively or negatively, have a massive impact on our mental, and therefore physical health. The relationship that Jesus had with us was physical, spiritual and mental; He came into this world as a human being. The resurrection was a physical event, so our relationship with God is at each of these levels. This is critical, as sin and the effects of sin operate at all these levels, but so does deliverance and healing.

One of the issues that arises in thinking about good and evil, and sin, is the possibility of dualism. Dualism is seeing good and evil as equal but opposite. This is not the biblical position. In the book of Job, Satan needs God's permission to attack (Job 1:12). If we go to creation, we see the earth is the Lord's, He made it, and humankind comes from His breath (Genesis 2:7). The psalms reiterate this view; for example, 'The earth is the LORD's, and everything in it' (Psalm 24:1). In John 1:5 we have the metaphor of light, which shines in the darkness and the darkness has not overcome it. Good is infinitely bigger than evil, because the source of life is God. This needs both cognitive and emotional recognition. Understanding and affirming with our minds is important but not enough, as our emotions also determine our response. I have never met Christians who believe God and Satan are equal, but I have often met Christians who act as though they are. For example, in conferences and in churches I have occasionally seen the deliverance ministry carried out at high volumes, which is indicative, I suspect, of the fear of the one ministering. It is also bad practice as it is never nice to be shouted at! It doesn't help that the language of the New Testament in this area can be quite martial in tone, and can easily be taken out of context. For example, in Ephesians 6, Paul is using the picture of a Roman soldier, with their belt, breastplate, shield, and sword. It is far too easy to avoid our fears with martial, warlike images and thoughts. This can be dangerous, as we can get so focused on the battle that we lose sight of who we are and who God is.

Potentially this makes us very vulnerable, as relationally we are compromised both within ourselves and with God; not to mention that our fears can break through at any point.

I don't believe that Paul had the picture of the Roman soldier in mind as a way of avoiding our fears. He starts that famous passage in Ephesians 6 with the words 'be strong in the Lord' (v.10), and ends it with 'keep on praying for all the Lord's people' (v.18). Our strength cognitively and emotionally is in the Lord. I may well have fears that get hooked in this area, but it is not my strength that is important; what is important is that I know I am in the Lord. So in practice what is needed is that before any ministry I am very honest with God about my fears. I do not avoid them; I place them into His hands. It is His strength I need. In Ephesians 6:10-14, the word 'stand' occurs four times. This is not about where I stand as me, but knowing I stand with the Lord: 'Finally, be strong in the Lord and in his mighty power' (v.10). Paul ends this great passage with the injunction to pray for all the saints and for him (v.19). We are joined together as the body of Christ, we are united with Christ at the head.

40

Chapter 3
Power

The power of Jesus

> 'The reason the Son of God appeared was to destroy the devil's work' (1 John 3:8).

The focal point for the triumph of Jesus is the place where there is the most failure – the cross. To get to the cross was an act of love seen in obedience (Luke 22:39-43). The cross is the focal point for all shame, for all abandonment, for all sin. Here Paul's words echo: 'For the wages of sin is death, but the gift of God is eternal life in Christ Jesus our Lord' (Romans 6:23). Here is the literal outworking of sin, death taken on by the one person for whom it was not deserved, the Son of God.

With the taking on and accepting of the price of sin, death had to happen in the most degrading form possible. But the act of acceptance by Jesus in such great love carried all sin into the heart of the Godhead. Jürgen Moltmann in his great book, *The Crucified God*[6] rightly, in my view, points out that the crucifixion hits in different ways the entire Trinity. The Spirit is devastated by powerlessness,

---

[6] Jürgen Moltmann, *The Crucified God* (London: SCM, 1974).

and the Father undergoes the agony of grief at the death of His Son.

Psychotherapists know that for a client to move on, to heal, they need a relationship with the therapist that is empathic, genuine and compassionate. Rarely is the word 'love' used, as it is in our world too overlaid with sexuality. But if sin and all its consequences, if evil with all its malevolence, is taken into the heart of the Godhead through death, it is met with the transformation of Trinitarian love, that of the Father for the Son, the Son for the Father, and the Spirit encompassing both.

Evil has at least three different focuses: humans are more than capable of harming each other; the demonic wants to break the relationship with God; and there is natural evil. Natural evil is all those things that work against relationship with God and cause harm as a result of living in a fallen world. It can be the political systems of society, it can be economics, it can be weather.

Such love which we see in the life of Christ now meets the mass of human, demonic and natural evil. Evil in all its forms, sin in all its forms, is met with acceptance, grace and compassion between the Father, Son and Spirit. Such acceptance transforms. This is the reality of the power of God.

The power of God in Jesus is seen with the sharpest focus in dealing with the demonic. Here we have in the most undiluted form, evil. The demonic is the most undiluted form of evil because it goes to the root of destroying the core of what it means to be human, namely living in relationship with God. This is seen with the tightest focus in Matthew 12:24-28 (and Luke 11:17-20), where Jesus is being challenged by the Pharisees over His deliverance ministry:

> But when the Pharisees heard this, they said, 'It is only by Beelzebul, the prince of demons, that this fellow drives out demons.'
>
> Jesus knew their thoughts and said to them, 'Every kingdom divided against itself will be ruined, and every city or household divided against itself will not stand. If Satan drives out Satan, he is divided against himself. How then can his kingdom stand? And if I drive out demons by Beelzebul, by whom do your people drive them out? So then, they will be your judges. But if it is by the Spirit of God that I drive out demons, then the kingdom of God has come upon you.'
> *Matthew 12:24-28*

For Jesus, exercising the power of the Spirit was the reality of the kingdom of God being here and now. Jesus saw getting rid of demons not just as casting out, or victory over Satan, but as binding all the powers of evil. This is what was promised at the end of the age; when Jesus comes again, all evil will be vanquished. But the incredible truth is that Jesus saw the end of the age as being now in the deliverance ministry. The kingdom of God was present because the Spirit of God was present, and this happened in and through Jesus and He moved in that power.

It is in this ministry of Jesus, and only in this ministry, that Jesus makes the assertion that the kingdom has come. This was a new and the final way of God operating. In this ministry there is no 'now but not yet' – the kingdom is here. This is an astonishing fact. In every other area of the ministry of Jesus, there is the dynamic of the kingdom coming but not being there in its fullness. For example, in His healing ministry, there is always the recognition that healing is in one sense temporary; death cannot be avoided, even for Lazarus eventually. In His ministry dealing with natural elements, such as the calming of the storm (Mark 4:39) these are signs of the kingdom, but not the fullness of the kingdom.

This puts the deliverance ministry of Jesus in a pivotal position; if we want to see what the kingdom of God looks like, here we have it revealed in its fullness. In the deliverance ministry of Jesus, the absolute power of the kingdom is shown as present now. This is why it is very dangerous to try to relegate the deliverance ministry to the sidelines of the Church. It is in this area and only in this area that the fullness of the kingdom is seen. If the Church takes this off the agenda, it undermines the whole authority of both the Church and Christ. The deliverance ministry is the prophetic statement of Jesus' ministry, in that as demons cannot stand, so it will be in the kingdom that sickness cannot stand, sin cannot stand. There will be a complete wholeness. But it is more than prophetic in the sense that it is from this ministry that the kingdom of God flows into the fallen world; with the fall of evil and Satan comes the restoration, and it starts here.

It is not easy to accept this. For example, in Mark 9:14-29, we have the deliverance of the boy with a deaf and dumb spirit. The symptoms that are described, gnashing of teeth, and foaming at the mouth, are very similar to certain forms of epilepsy. This has led some commentators to say that really Jesus was healing epilepsy, not casting out an evil spirit. What is true is that the boy was healed, but by (according to the text) deliverance from an evil spirit. Jesus was quite clear in His ministry in what needed physical healing and what needed deliverance.

In Mark 3:29 and Matthew 12:32, we have the saying of the unforgiveable sin, 'but whoever blasphemes against the Holy Spirit will never be forgiven; they are guilty of an eternal sin' (Mark 3:29). In both Matthew and Mark this is associated with the Beelzebul controversy. As James Dunn points out in *Jesus and the Spirit*,[7] Jesus is saying that

> To reject or deny the power he displayed was to put the critic beyond forgiveness! ... In him, in his action (in the dealing with demons) God was present and active in a decisive and final way – to reject his ministry was to reject God and so to reject forgiveness.

Recently, I was speaking at a training conference for Church of England ministers, and afterwards one minister came up to me, and said, 'So if you take out the deliverance ministry of Jesus, you in effect take out all His ministry.' I had never heard it put quite so bluntly, but yes, that is the case I believe, biblically and in practice.

---

[7] James Dunn, *Jesus and the Spirit* (London: SCM, 1975) p.53.

The power of the children of God

For Jesus, His ministry was the exercising of the power of the Spirit. It is the movement and outpouring of the Spirit that gives the continuity and power from Jesus to us. We move in the power of the Spirit. The great prophecy of Joel is now here (Joel 2:28-32). The Spirit has been poured out on all people (Acts 2:17-21).

If we move in the power of the Spirit of God that has been poured upon us, what Jesus says starts to make more sense. Jesus said, 'Very truly I tell you, whoever believes in me will do the works I have been doing, and they will do even greater things than these, because I am going to the Father' (John 14:12).

This has to be true because all of us can move in the power of the Spirit. This is not cheap triumphalism, though, for as the life of Christ shows us, this is a battle. To move in the power of the Spirit is a call to radical discipleship. Throughout history there have been great movements of the Spirit, normally preceded by prayer and repentance. In the Western world there is little doubt that we are potentially heavily compromised by our consumerism and drive for comfort. It is very easy to slot faith into something that makes us feel good or better, and fail to see the radical call to life that it really is.

The power of the Spirit working through us happens through being in relationship with Jesus through the Spirit. This can have dramatic high points, such as baptism in the Spirit, but in the longer term relies on an ever-deepening relationship, growing in trust and love. This is not without risk. I love the passage in Matthew 14:22-33, where Peter

46

walks on the water towards Jesus. It has always struck me that to walk on water you have to face the reality of the fear of drowning. Following Christ means living in relationship with Him, and above all, as Peter discovered, keeping your focus on Him, because it is only from within the relationship that you can face and overcome the fears.

As human beings we evolve systems and develop ways of doing things because they work. For example, there are ways of fixing a car, and you need to know the rules and follow them. In the deliverance ministry it does not work by rules but by relationship with Christ. Within any relationship there are guidelines that need to be followed if the relationship is to flourish; for example, you need to spend time with someone to know them. But the guidelines are there to enhance the relationship and are not aims or goals in themselves.

There are considerable dangers in trying to do things by a formula, or by law:

> Some Jews who went around driving out evil spirits tried to invoke the name of the Lord Jesus over those who were demon-possessed. They would say, 'In the name of the Jesus whom Paul preaches, I command you to come out.' Seven sons of Sceva, a Jewish chief priest, were doing this. One day the evil spirit answered them, 'Jesus I know, and Paul I know about, but who are you?' Then the man who had the evil spirit jumped on them and overpowered them all. He gave them such a beating that they ran out of the house naked and bleeding.
> *Acts 19:13-16*

The power of the children of God is relationship-based, as it is through the relationship the Spirit of God operates. The sons of Sceva were not in relationship either with Jesus or Paul. They were just using a formula.

For Jesus, though, the relationship with the Father was not limited to the two of them. It was expressed in the love that He had for you and me. Likewise, the relationship with God we have as individuals is not just for us but for one another.

Jesus is clear that the relationship with Himself has to be shared to be real. So for example, He says: 'A new command I give you: love one another. As I have loved you, so you must love one another. By this everyone will know that you are my disciples, if you love one another' (John 13:34-35). This gives a slightly different relational dynamic that the early Church was well aware of. For example, John writes: 'Anyone who claims to be in the light but hates a brother or sister is still in the darkness' (1 John 2:9). Paul in 1Corinthians 12:12ff uses the analogy of a body to express the interrelationship we have with Christ and each other. So we move in the power of the Spirit that is relationally dependent both on our personal relationship with Christ and with each other.

We need to honour this. Power has the capacity to corrupt, and this is why the power of the risen Lord, through the Spirit, is not an individual thing. It is given to the individual but in the context of the body of Christ. Although in recent decades there has been a massive rediscovery of the works of the Holy Spirit, sometimes the emphasis has been too much on the individual. This has played into the Western cult of celebrity, sometimes with devastating results, both for the 'celebrity' and others. You receive the baptism in the Spirit as an individual, but the Spirit works through the body.

Because, in this ministry, the power of the Spirit is absolutely here, the kingdom of God has come, we need to walk with humility and holiness. The most fertile ground for evil is that which is produced through disunity, fracture and broken relationships, especially within the Church, as this compromises the integrity of the body of Christ. This is not a cry for uniformity but a plea for the unity of believers centred on the cross.

The power of the demonic

In the Old Testament (Genesis 3:1ff; Zechariah 3:1; Job 1:6ff, 1 Chronicles 21:1), Satan, or the serpent, is seen as having three roles. Firstly, that of the tempter, for Adam and Eve. Secondly, that of the accuser in Zechariah. Thirdly in Job, being allowed by God to cause considerable harm and upset to Job. In Chronicles, Satan is seen again as the one who incites to sin, the tempter.

In the New Testament the role of Satan, Beelzebul, the devil, and evil spirits is expanded. We have Satan as the tempter at the beginning of Christ's ministry (Matthew 4:1-11; Luke 4:1-13; Mark 1:12-13). In Luke 13:16 we have Satan as keeping someone bound and crippled. In Luke 22:3 Satan enters Judas. In Corinthians Satan is seen as the deceiver who 'masquerades as an angel of light' (2 Corinthians 11:14). In 1 Peter 5:8 Satan is seen as a roaring lion waiting to devour those he can.

If you look at evil spirits, in 1 Samuel 16:14 an evil spirit is sent by God to torment Saul. In Luke chapters 7 and 8, evil spirits are cast out by Jesus, as in Mark chapters 3, 5 and 9. Spirits are sometimes identified by the characteristics they produce, for example in Mark 9:25, the deaf and mute spirit.

The biblical picture is firstly one of the supreme authority of God. Satan and every evil spirit are subject to the authority of God. In Luke 9:1 authority is given by Jesus to the Twelve to deal with evil spirits. In Luke 10:17 we have the same authority given to the 72. In the Mark version of the commissioning of the Twelve (Mark 6:7), we again have the same authority given.

The role of Satan and evil spirits is to cause us to separate from our relationship with God by sinning. This is the key aspect seen both in Genesis and the temptations of Jesus. This is why the Lord's Prayer is so specific, 'lead us not into temptation, but deliver us from … evil' (Matthew 6:13). Sin separates from God, and as a result separates us from the life that God has for us. Even with temptation we are promised the help of God. In Hebrews we read:

> For we do not have a high priest who is unable to feel sympathy for our weaknesses, but we have one who has been tempted in every way, just as we are – yet he did not sin. Let us then approach God's throne of grace with confidence, so that we may receive mercy and find grace to help us in our time of need.
> *Hebrews 4:15-16*

Or in other words, in temptation we can approach God and ask for help.

Demons have the power to cause physical illness. In Jesus' ministry He cast out demons often just using the symptoms they cause. But it is wrong to automatically attribute illness to sin or the demonic:

> As he went along, he saw a man blind from birth. His disciples asked him, 'Rabbi, who sinned, this man or his parents, that he would be born blind?'
> 'Neither this man nor his parents sinned,' said Jesus, 'but this happened so that the works of God might be displayed in him.'
> *John 9:1-3*

But it is interesting to note that in the commissioning of the disciples and the 72, healing and deliverance from evil spirits go hand in hand, as it does in the Mark version of the Great Commission. It is perhaps right that it is not easy to draw clean lines between the two, and sometimes they are connected.

This means that in every situation there has to be discernment and dependence on God, to know what is happening. This is particularly true in the deliverance ministry, as rarely are situations simple. They may well involve elements not just of the demonic but also of sin, and the need for healing in its different forms.

52

Chapter 4
Discernment

One of the most difficult but essential things to be able to do is to be able to discern what is actually going on with a situation – is it demonic, is it psychological, is it physical, is it all these things, and what is the right thing to do now? One of the important things for knowing what is occurring is being aware of all the different aspects of a situation. Sometimes the failure to have a broad picture can result in not being able to hear what God wants to do, or what is really going on. The more my vision is limited, the less likely I am to see what is really happening.

A few years ago I was at an evangelistic conference, and had been asked to keep an eye on the deliverance ministry. This was easier said than done, as there were many different churches involved, from a wide variety of denominations. At the time of ministry at the end, I saw two people volubly and loudly 'casting out' demons from a lad who was no more than 14 years old. Now, laying aside for a minute the whole issue of whether this was appropriate in this setting with someone of this age, I decided that I really needed to intervene. The boy seemed be to acting as though the demonic was present, but something felt very wrong. The boy was constantly glancing at his friend who was standing about five metres away. The boy was faking it for a joke. Unfortunately, the people praying for him did not realise what was going on. They were so caught in a narrow picture of what the deliverance ministry was, that they were fooled by a young boy. He thought it was a great joke, I was less amused, and those praying simply looked foolish.

Evil comes from at least three sources:

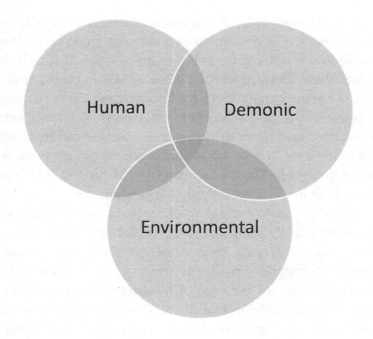

Satan and the demonic is the clearest expression of evil, because here we have breakdown of the relationship with God in the most obvious terms. Evil is the intention to separate us from God and break the relationship with Him. Sin is the response to evil that causes the separation.

Evil can also be human in origin. We have an incredible capacity to be evil to one another, to promote selfishness and harm each other. Likewise, sometimes the environment, society and the natural world can be evil, and our response to such evil can be sinful. Sometimes because it simply seems the norm. Consumerism is at one level evil, as it promotes the concept that things bring happiness and fulfilment, not relationships. So the aim in life is not to seek relationships with God and each other, but rather to accumulate wealth.

Understanding where evil originates from is important, as different types of ministry may be required. For example, often human evil is the result of things that have happened to a person in childhood, and therefore it is a nonsense to try to cast the demonic out, as it is not there. Having said that, though, there is often an interrelationship between the different sources of evil, and they can overlap. In environmental terms we see this in the whole thinking about territorial spirits. Territorial spirits are presumed to be where areas and populations have a particular sense of oppression, and the spirit feeds and holds onto this oppression. The oppression can be due to economics, or social dynamics.

Evil is rarely simple! So this ministry needs to have a holistic approach, not necessarily from one person, but certainly from the Church in the widest sense. Any deliverance ministry needs to recognise the breadth of evil. In our local group of churches (the Diocese of Lichfield) we will only accept referrals for the deliverance ministry if they come through the area minister (the vicar). This is because we recognise that this ministry will need at least some form of ongoing pastoral care, so there have to be links to a local church.

Evil acts on us in a variety of ways that we need to recognise:

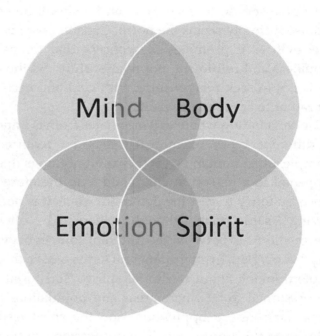

Evil can act on our thoughts (mind), and our bodies (for example, the demon-possessed man in Luke 8:26ff), our emotions (anger, hatred) and our spirits. And often the effects of evil are felt in a variety of ways, not just in one. The demon-possessed man in Luke's account was obviously affected in all these ways; it affected him in totality. The Jewish understanding of being human was holistic and these areas were not defined as being separate, but simply talked about individually as a point of emphasis, not separation. So when Paul talks about the flesh and the spirit in Galatians 5:17, he is not talking about separate bits of himself, but different points of focus. Everything is interrelated.

It is in this somewhat confusing context that discernment operates.

We see discernment as a gift in Corinthians – 'distinguishing between spirits' (1 Corinthians 12:10). The gift of discernment of spirits is given by God to an individual to use within the context of the Christian community (like every other gift). It is the capacity to know what is what, in a way that is based not just on human wisdom. It is a gift given not as something one owns, but as something that is exercised in the context of the relationship with God and each other. Discernment of spirits is given so that the work of God may be done. The gift of discernment of spirits may be given as a one-off in a situation, or a person may have the gift in a more permanent way.

What I find slightly odd is that discernment of spirits as a gift is not given more prominence in the New Testament, and it may be that within the early Church clear boundaries were seen in this area. For example:

> Therefore I want you to know that no one who is speaking by the Spirit of God says, 'Jesus be cursed,' and no one can say, 'Jesus is Lord,' except by the Holy Spirit.
> *1 Corinthians 12:3*
>
> Dear friends, do not believe every spirit, but test the spirits to see whether they are from God, because many false prophets have gone out into

the world. This is how you can recognise the
Spirit of God: every spirit that acknowledges that
Jesus Christ has come in the flesh is from God,
but every spirit that does not acknowledge Jesus
is not from God.
1 John 4:1-3

Given that the early Church was much more aware of
this area than we tend to be, it could just be that the gift of
discernment of spirits was seen as normal within the life of
the Church, and needed little or no emphasis. Certainly the
context of the early Church is one where opposition to the
gospel was clearly seen, theologically, politically and
socially.

Discernment, though, is not limited to spirits; it was part
of the whole life of Jesus. He knew what needed healing,
He knew what needed casting out, He knew who needed
compassion. This was a function not of a specific gift as
such, but more as knowledge rooted in the reality of the
relationship with the Father.

We see how this works in John chapter 5:

For this reason they tried all the more to kill him;
not only was he breaking the Sabbath, but he was
even calling God his own Father, making himself
equal with God.

Jesus gave them this answer: 'Very truly I tell
you, the Son can do nothing by himself; he can do
only what he sees his Father doing, because
whatever the Father does the Son also does. For
the Father loves the Son and shows him all he

does. Yes, and he will show him even greater
works than these, so that you will be amazed.'
John 5:18-20

In this passage Jesus was doing two things that were
absolutely forbidden by the religious leaders of the day.
Firstly, He was breaking the Sabbath. Now, in our society
that may not seem like a big deal; we do not have those
kind of laws. But for the Jewish religious leaders, it was a
huge thing to do. The law defined the identity and value
not only of the individual but of the nation. So what Jesus
was doing was challenging the identity and foundation of
their beings. This was extremely threatening and
dangerous in the eyes of the Jewish leaders. They were the
guardians of the law that was seen as something that God
Himself had ordained. So Jesus was putting Himself above
something God had put into place. Secondly, He was
calling God His Father and making Himself equal with
God. This was the ultimate blasphemy and punishable by
death. Jesus is changing the whole system – not just
adjusting it, but taking out the key point of reference. For
the Jewish leaders, the point of reference was the God-
given law, but Jesus is saying that from now on the point
of reference is the relationship you have with the Father;
one that is not mediated any longer by law, but by the life-
giving relating to God to which we are called.

This has profound consequences for the deliverance
ministry. Human beings love law! Law tells us how to do
things. If I am baking a cake, I follow the instructions! But
the deliverance ministry is not about law. There are
guidelines – these are not laws, but pointers to the
relational. It is very easy to subtly substitute law for

relating to God. For example, it is tempting to say, 'I know that we have authority in Christ over demons, so all I have to do is stand in that authority and cast them out.' No, that is law-based, not relational to God or the person being ministered to. I might well miss what God actually wants to do, I could well fail to hear what the other person is saying. This ministry is above all relational and that comes first. It is not that I am wrong to think that Christ has authority, but I am wrong to apply that as law, and fail to see it in the context of relationship with Him.

This means that our preparation for ministry in this area needs closer scrutiny. I need to ask myself certain questions: how is my walk with Christ? I will always remember ministering to somebody with a more senior clergy person. I arrived early to be briefed, but I was not prepared for what then happened. My senior colleague said to me, 'Would you hear my confession?' I was a little thrown by this, as liturgical confession was not in my evangelical theology, but muddled my way through. I was deeply moved and challenged by the vulnerability and honesty of my colleague. Jesus did what He saw the Father doing. For me to see what God is doing, my relationship with Him has to be clear, I need to face myself, and be prepared to clear my decks. To say that this can be uncomfortable is an understatement, as I need to, as far as I can, face my weaknesses, know my vulnerabilities, and bring them into the presence, love and protection of Christ. I am always a work in progress, but for the love and protection of Jesus I need to own those areas before Him. Knowing one's weaknesses, owning one's sin, is a prerequisite for this ministry.

It may well be this issue that Jesus is addressing with His disciples in Mark 9:29, when He says this kind can only come out by prayer and fasting. Prayer and fasting draw us into the presence of God, opening us up to His loving care, enabling us to face our sin and weaknesses. One of the great strengths of liturgical confession is that you do not do it alone, and you do it in the safety of absolute confidentiality. The relational dynamic of loving God and being with someone else is critical. How this is worked out in different churches and denominations will vary, but the principles hold true for this ministry.

If we hold the point of reference as Christ, then we avoid some of the pitfalls that we know in the dynamics of human relationships. Human beings have the capacity to pick up each other's emotions. How this works is not entirely clear, but it is thought that mirror neurones play a part in this. We literally can feel what the other person is feeling, but understand it through our own filters of experience and knowledge. In the ministry scenario, people can be very vulnerable and open, so it is very easy to pick up the other person's emotions. Sometimes I have interpreted this as a word from God, and seen others do the same. Nothing could be further from the truth.

If my point of reference is Christ, all the time I need to be asking Him what is going on, where do we go next, in the ministry scenario. It is a little bit like a three-way conversation, between the person being ministered to, God and myself. This has a parallel in secular psychotherapy or counselling, as the internal supervisor. Here constantly there are checks going on: is what I feel my personal interpretation, etc? This is not an easy scenario, as the brain easily gets distracted or engrossed in one conversation to the detriment of the other! So it is worth sometimes internally to say, 'Stop, am I losing sight of the person in front of me? Am I listening to God in all of this?'

This ministry has to be done within the love and character of Jesus. Love, support and challenge are all part of how Jesus deals with us; for example, the rich young ruler. In Matthew 19:16-22, Jesus affirms and supports the young man by giving him the commandments that He knows he has kept, then challenges him with selling what he possesses.

How Jesus deals with the demonic is clear: with straight authority. There is little ceremony, and no messing around. This is important, as sometimes I have seen ministry in this area as loud, full of drama, and have come away thinking I would be more traumatised by the ministry style than the demonic!

If we hold the relational nature of discernment, we avoid the psychic. Some people have the capacity to just know what is happening in another person, and this is sometimes labelled as being psychic.[8] In my experience this is rarely beneficial to the person who knows, or to the person who is being told. If we hold to relational dynamic of this ministry with Christ, this can be avoided. At the constant centre is Jesus; what is He saying? I have come across circumstances where this has got confused, and people who are psychic are on deliverance teams, because others have thought they have the gift of discernment. This rarely works out well.

---

[8] Many Christians, however, believe 'psychic' gifts are demonic in origin – that is, never natural.

Two of the key guidelines in discernment are knowledge and common sense. With the huge growth in knowledge about human mental health problems, there is a wealth of knowledge that is useful. That is not to say everyone needs to be an expert in mental health, but it is to say that some of the basics need to be borne in mind. There are three main areas that in my experience are important.

Firstly, the person who is so wounded that they crave attention. Occasionally individuals have suffered such neglect and abandonment that they have a need for attention at any cost. They occasionally come for deliverance ministry, as it is a place where there is a great deal of attention paid to the individual. It is also because the deliverance ministry is an excellent place for them to project their fears and angers. The really key issue here is that the ministry is never enough, there is always more, always something else; occasionally they can be very demanding, because they are hurting so much. Very clear boundaries are needed by those involved in this ministry. For example, I will never go at night to pray with someone; I will always go with someone else; etc. The capacity to say no, not now, firmly but caringly is critical.

Secondly, dissociative disorders. This is where someone has experienced such a high level of emotional and/or physical abuse that to contain the pain and the trauma they almost have to split it off in their mind. But under certain conditions it can resurface. When different parts of the human personality surface they can have different voices and mannerisms. To experience this can be very odd, and it is tempting perhaps to think that it is a demon speaking to you. It is not a demon, though, it is part of that person.

To cast it out is potentially very damaging for the person involved, as it is saying that part of them is not acceptable. To avoid this, listening carefully to someone's background is important. Take time to listen to the story.

The extreme of this is Dissociative Identity Disorder (DID), where there can be almost completely separate personalities. Irrespective of whether the person has been involved in the occult or not, if this is present there is absolutely no point in doing deliverance, because all that happens is that aspect of the person's personality temporarily disappears. But of course it has not gone away. All involved in the deliverance ministry have a duty of care to those they minister to. That duty of care is given by Jesus. Discernment is knowing what God wants to do for this person now, and sometimes that may well mean signposting them to other forms of pastoral care or healing. Similar to DID in appearance (but not cause), is the whole area of psychotic disorders which includes various forms of schizophrenia. Hearing voices does not mean, necessarily, that deliverance is needed.

Thirdly, medication can cause hallucinations. Some years ago I had a lovely, deeply spiritual man in my church. Stan was in his seventies, and always supported what the church was doing. However, he was diagnosed with Parkinson's disease and given the appropriate medication. It was a troubling time as he began to see people appearing in his living room. Naturally he asked that we would come and pray in his house. So we did so, in the main praying for peace, and cleansing his home. After we prayed in his house peace came, but then the symptoms came back after two weeks. This was a little puzzling, but in those two weeks a little bit of research showed that the drugs he was taking could give rise to hallucinations. So he went back to his doctor and had his medication changed. This resolved the issue. It was as if God gave him peace for the two weeks so that the issue could be resolved medically.

Using common sense in this ministry is key. The demonic is not omnipresent, so if it is there, there has to be a very good reason. It may be that there has been involvement in the occult, it may be that the person involved has been targeted for some reason – use wisdom.

Listen carefully to those you are ministering to, and do not engage in this ministry if you are not in a good place with God yourself. Make sure that you are able to maintain appropriate boundaries, and have support for yourself. We will look at this more in Chapter 10.

Key pointers for discernment

- Keep an honest relationship with Christ, owning your weaknesses.

- Make sure that you are not ministering alone; this is a ministry that always needs two.

- Do not be afraid to delay.

- Make sure that you feel grounded, are not tired, and are able to pay attention to God and the person. (If in doubt, or not in a good place, delay the ministry.)

- Keep an open mind; do not jump to conclusions.

- Do not let the person being ministered to set the agenda, or in other words, tell you what to do.

- Honour your doubts, if you have them, and do not be afraid to revisit a question, asking the person to clarify if necessary.

- Ask if there has been involvement with the occult, or if there is any reason why they may have been targeted.

Chapter 5
Cursing

Relating in the kingdom of God

It is uncomfortable to think about the evil that human beings do to each other. Wars, greed, abuse are all part of the human story. In more recent history the Holocaust, the Rwandan genocide and the Syrian conflict stand out as focal points. Despite being formed by the breath of God, our capacity for evil has few limits.

This was no different in Jesus' day. Israel was under Roman occupation, and suffered all the abuses of being an occupied nation, along with a governing religious structure that was oppressive and abusive. But what kind of society was Jesus envisaging? What did the coming kingdom of God mean for human society? How was this to be played out in practice?

To understand what Jesus had in mind, we have to look at how He went about it. Firstly, He chose a mix of disciples that was a recipe for conflict: a tax collector, a political radical, conservative fishermen. The kingdom is going to have all sorts in it, and getting along with each other is going to mean losing preconceived ideas as to who is acceptable and who is not. It must have been hard for some of the disciples to accept Matthew, a tax collector. The only way forward for such a volatile mix of people is that they have a clear common goal and are committed to it. Their focus has to be the same, and the common factor that they all share is Jesus. The issues and desires they have as being human have not gone away, but now they have to be worked out in the context of their relationship with Jesus. James and John, for example, have a love of power, but this has to come to be worked out with Christ, not apart from Him (Mark 10:35-40).

Secondly, the disciples were removed from their homes. Their place of safety was for some the fishing village, but when Jesus calls them, He calls them to a situation where they are going to have to depend on Him and each other above everything else: 'the Son of Man has nowhere to lay his head ... No one who puts a hand to the plough and looks back is fit for service in the kingdom of God' (Luke 9:58ff). This is incredibly radical for the disciples. They were used to the support of family and community and indeed depended on it; that is where their loyalties lay. Now they are going to have to hold these loyalties as secondary to the primary loyalty of following and trusting Christ. In Mark's Gospel this is emphasised by Jesus: 'Then he looked at those seated in a circle round him and said, "Here are my mother and my brothers! Whoever does God's will is my brother and sister and mother"' (Mark 3:34-35).

Within human society today two polarities are seen: firstly, individualism, whereby I see myself as the arbiter and focal point of life, and secondly, tribalism, where my personal identity is a function of the community. Jesus points another way forward, personal in that my relationship with Him is something I experience and know through the Spirit, and communal in that my experience of God is worked out and known through loving my brother and sister. But in both cases the focal point is the same, the person of Jesus, as it was for the disciples.

It is no surprise then that Jesus has some clear teaching on how His followers are to relate:

> A new command I give you: love one another. As
> I have loved you, so you must love one another.
> By this everyone will know that you are my
> disciples, if you love one another.
> *John 13:34-35*

This is the defining principle for the relationships in the kingdom: loving like Jesus did. But this has consequences; the way the Church loves will be the witness to the world. The most powerful dynamic in human existence is the relationships we experience; it is these that determine our brain structure, our joys, our despairs. In the kingdom, the dynamic of love is the most healing experience that we can know as human beings. We see this most clearly on the cross, but this love is to be seen in our relationships with each other. No wonder the relationships of the kingdom are the most powerful witness to Christ.

Relational dynamics

Jesus was well aware of the power and effect of emotion in human relationships:

> But I tell you that anyone who is angry with a
> brother or sister will be subject to judgment.

> Again, anyone who says to a brother or sister, 'Raca,' is answerable to the court. And anyone who says, 'You fool!' will be in danger of the fire of hell.
>
> *Matthew 5:22*

He was also aware that we easily fall short, and need forgiveness (as seen in the Lord's Prayer).

In the early Church this took some outworking and thinking about. Paul saw the interrelationship of the Church as the body of Christ (1 Corinthians 12:12ff), but he was constantly struggling with the relationships in the churches (1 Corinthians 3ff). This is a challenge that has not gone away. It is perhaps the greatest challenge for the Western Church today: how do we love each other; how do we relate?

The contribution of secular psychotherapy to the understanding and dynamics of relationships in the last 100 or so years has been profound. I was listening recently to a BBC Radio 4 programme, *Beyond Belief*,[9] where three psychotherapists were looking at the interrelationship of faith and psychotherapy. Perhaps one of the most interesting points made was that when the monasteries were destroyed, the Christian faith turned away from the contemplative practices that were in the monasteries. The result of this was that faith stopped being something that engaged with my deep fears and anxieties. It became much more something that I did as an external process, not realising or understanding that this had profound consequences for my internal dynamics. I remember that

---

[9] 4th January 2016.

when I became a Christian, the really important factor that was stressed to me was to read my Bible daily. I had absolutely no teaching on how the relationship with Jesus was going to develop, how I was going to engage emotionally. I was given a lot of things I ought to do.

This movement away from the inner journey meant losing a rich and diverse tradition, such as Ignatian spirituality and the Works of St John of the Cross, to name but two, but fortunately in recent years we are rediscovering these lost treasures. Every relationship has a dual dynamic; we look to the other, but we also look to ourselves as to the effect the other has, and how to relate back. We cannot lose either part.

In psychotherapy it has long been recognised that our interactions with each other have a profound effect. This is especially true when we are very young, and in our relationship with our primary caregiver. In later life the effects we have on each other can be no less dramatic. Who has not lain awake at night consumed by anxiety and fear because of an interaction we had with someone earlier in the day?

How we build up or knock down one another is seen in the Bible with the dynamics of cursing and blessing. Curses bring harm and damage; blessings bring healing and wholeness. This can be a conscious or subconscious act; sometimes we simply do not know what we are doing and the effect that it is having. Likewise, cursing or blessing does not have to be verbal, sometimes it can be just a look, or body language.

Generally, how we interact with one another can be upbuilding (a blessing), neutral or negative (a curse).

Emotions carry energy and provoke reactions. Fear can mobilise a fight or flight response. Anger can be experienced as something physical. The mechanisms for this are not clear.

It is no coincidence that behind blessing there is the tremendously powerful force of love, likewise with curses there is the energy and power of anger, and pain. Cursing and blessing in human terms comes with the power of these emotions. This is not a vague power but a powerfully focused energy which can influence other people for good or bad. One of the responsibilities that one has as a church leader is to lead meetings of various sorts. If all the members of the meeting come with a negative attitude it has an effect, and can be very hard to move forward positively. If, however, everyone comes positively, the outcome is very different. This is the power of emotion, and how it affects all of us. When emotion is verbalised it is conscious, and this is the reason we read in James 3:1-12 the dire warnings about the tongue. 'Likewise, the tongue is a small part of the body, but it makes great boasts. Consider what a great forest is set on fire by a small spark' (James 3:5).

One of the ways emotion is placed on another is by projection, but projection only happens if there is a genuine reason. I may experience rejection by someone else, but this can then allow all my unresolved pain and anger of rejection from the past to be projected onto that person. If you are on the receiving end of someone else's projection, this can be very unpleasant. The dynamics of emotions and how we experience them from others is the underlying dynamic of blessing and cursing. The warning in James, and seriousness with which Jesus took these dynamics, needs to be recognised. Jesus worked it through with the disciples; we need to work it through with each other. Working it through is full of tensions: on the one hand there is the emotion that is valid, and healing is required; on the other hand there is the need for the individual to own their emotion so that they can receive healing and not place it on someone else. This can only happen if we feel safe and accepted, and for the Church this means the focus on Jesus and His love is the priority above all else. It is only Christ who can give that safety of love.

The biblical witness

In the Bible we find that God engages in both blessing and cursing. Behind His blessing is His tremendous love, behind His cursing is His holy anger.

According to *The NIV Complete Concordance*,[10] in the Old Testament there are about 173 references to cursing, and 250 references to do with blessing. In the New Testament there are 26 references to do with cursing, and 77 references to do with blessing. (This depends a little on how you count them!)

The fundamental principle of cursing is found in Proverbs: 'Like a fluttering sparrow or a darting swallow, an undeserved curse does not come to rest' (Proverbs 26:2). This means that a curse that has no grounds of validity is totally ineffective. The grounds for validity in terms of a curse coming on a Christian individual or group is sin. If a

[10] *The NIV Complete Concordance* (Nashville, TN: Zondervan, 1981).

person is vulnerable because of their sin in that specific curse-targeted area, and engaged in promoting the kingdom of God, God may allow the curse to take hold.

This principle is seen in Numbers 5:11-31. A woman (who is part of the community of Israel) accused of adultery is tested by being cursed:

> If she has made herself impure and been unfaithful to her husband, this will be the result: when she is made to drink the water that brings a curse and causes bitter suffering, it will enter her, her abdomen will swell and her womb will miscarry, and she will become a curse.
> *Numbers 5:27*

God Himself curses in specific situations; for example, in Genesis God curses the serpent. Why? 'Because you have done this' (Genesis 3:14), i.e. caused Adam and Eve to sin. But it does not stop there. Adam and Eve are also cursed for the sin they have committed, Eve to pain in childbearing (Genesis 3:16), Adam to 'painful toil' (Genesis 3:17-19). Curses are the opposite of blessings, and in Deuteronomy this is laid out before the Israelites:

> See I am setting before you today a blessing and a curse – the blessing if you obey the commands of the LORD your God that I am giving you today; the curse if you disobey the commands of the LORD your God and turn from the way that I command you today by following other gods, which you have not known.
> *Deuteronomy 11:26-28*

How we should respond to cursing is by blessing. 'Bless those who persecute you; bless and do not curse' (Romans 12:14). 'When we are cursed, we bless' (1 Corinthians 4:12). This has to be the case, as the core of our relationship with Christ is love. God Himself is defined as love at one point: 'Whoever does not love does not know God, because God is love' (1 John 4:8). However, this can have an interesting effect as Paul notes in Romans:

> Do not take revenge, my dear friends, but leave room for God's wrath, for it is written: 'It is mine to avenge; I will repay,' says the Lord. On the contrary:
> 'If your enemy is hungry, feed him;
> if he is thirsty, give him something to drink.
> In doing this, you will heap burning coals on his head.'
> *Romans 12:19-20*

When blessing and cursing involve God and the demonic, there is an added dimension over and above human dynamics. With God, we often pray His blessing and love over others, and in doing so we are invoking not just our own love, but His as well. It is exactly the same with cursing and the demonic, except the emotions are negative and destructive.

Demonic cursing

Curses have their root in anger. With God it is holy anger, but there is also ungodly anger, the anger that wishes sinful personal destruction on some person or place. This sinful anger is hatred and is at the core of demonic cursing.

Demonic cursing is the intense wishing of evil upon a person or group of people, empowered by the energy of hatred and anger focused upon the person or group. It can involve a deliberate intention to involve the demonic, through satanic ritual activity. The involvement of the demonic may, however, have been unwittingly invoked by the hatred and anger, as that is the emotional currency of the demonic.

We know from those who have left satanic cults that those who take part in satanic ritual activities seek to increase the energy used in the process of cursing by generating pain and fear in their victims as part of their cultic rituals. They wish to draw off the energy so created and use it to further empower the curses and also to enhance their sense of well-being. The demonic powers are specifically invoked to further empower the curse. A very similar mechanism exists within witchcraft, the 'cone of power', that is used for spells.

Those who have been at the receiving end of a demonic curse know that it can be a distressing experience. We ourselves have noted that strangely it seems to vary in intensity. Sometimes when a curse is particularly intense, reference to the curse as being empowered by human sacrifice has been the key to release.

Andrew Boyd helps us to see a possible reason for this:

> The understanding behind occultic ritual sacrifice stems from the belief that the life force is in the blood. The death of a person or animal is believed to release energy to please or appease

> Satan or another entity and give power to the
> celebrants. Energy is also believed to be released
> by pain, hence the allegations of the ritual torture
> of animals.[11]

He further relates the stories of three people who claim to be survivors of ritual abuse.[12] These accounts are unverified, yet they each speak of human sacrifice in the three separate groups that they were involved with. Anyone who reads the large amount of literature available today describing the experiences of those who have been members of groups which engage in ritual sacrifice will be aware of the frequent reference to human as well as animal sacrifice. It therefore does not seem too fanciful to believe that we are dealing with real situations when we address the issue of curses placed upon others and upon ourselves which used human ritual sacrifice as a means to empower the curse.

In all of this, though, we must not lose sight of the fact that God is in charge. Paul's great statement of faith is as valid now as it was then:

> No, in all these things we are more than
> conquerors through him who loved us. For I am
> convinced that neither death nor life, neither
> angels nor demons, neither the present nor the
> future, nor any powers, neither height nor depth,
> nor anything else in all creation, will be able to
> separate us from the love of God that is in Christ
> Jesus our Lord.

---

[11] *Blasphemous Rumours*, p.122.
[12] ibid., pp.321ff.

We see this in the case of Balaam: 'How can I curse those whom God has not cursed? How can I denounce those whom the LORD has not denounced?' (Numbers 23:8). King David recognises the principle of God's sovereignty in 2 Samuel 16:5-14. He is going along the road and is cursed by Shimei in very specific and deadly terms. 'The LORD has given the kingdom into the hands of your son Absalom. You have come to ruin because you are a murderer!' (v.8). The reaction of one of his followers is equally direct: 'Why should this dead dog curse my lord the king? Let me go over and cut off his head' (v.9). David replies, 'Leave him alone; let him curse, for the LORD has told him to' (v.11).

Shimei then continues cursing David, pelting him with stones and dirt all the way to Jerusalem. The result is that they arrive, we are told, 'exhausted' (v.14). The exhaustion may have been simply due to the effort of getting there, but one of the most common effects of being under a curse is exhaustion, a feeling of being totally drained. In terms of demonic cursing, this is particularly experienced in the two-week run-up to the satanic festivals. In conversations with those who have been involved in satanic groups, this is because churches that worship God and are moving in the Spirit impact spiritually the area around them. The aim of cursing in this instance is to try to paralyse the church prior to the festival. This has become such a regular feature in our church that we have a specific prayer group that deals with these events.

In the Church

The dynamics of cursing and blessing involve both the emotional and spiritual. Because we are all human, these dynamics also happen within the Church. Particularly it can be focused on leaders, as they are the most obvious people on whom to project. They are authority figures and sometimes parental figures, as a result of which they will be subject to the emotional and spiritual dynamics of others. What is particularly noticeable is that this gets worse at times when God is blessing. This is because as the love of God is poured out, more hurts and pains come to the surface, as for the individual it is safe to start facing them. Often, though, the church is not equipped or aware of what is happening, so instead of dealing with the issues pastorally and helping people to see their own agendas and wounds, conflict can erupt. I do wonder how many church splits could be avoided if this dynamic was recognised and engaged with. As mentioned earlier in the chapter, part of being able to deal with these dynamics is to have safety. Jesus made it safe for His disciples to address the issues they needed to, and we need to make it safe for each other, by keeping the focus on Christ, and being prepared to walk with each other, without judgement and with compassion.

All of this begs the question, why does God allow it? Curses take hold in our places of weaknesses. So cursing exposes the places where I need healing, where I need to face fears and hurts. So, paradoxically, cursing opens up the potential for healing and wholeness.

How do you know that you have been cursed?

Discernment, as discussed in Chapter 4, is key. With cursing, what is particularly important is to be able to know what is normal to feel, and what is abnormal. For example, was there a reason to feel very depressed, or have I picked up a curse, projection, emotion from someone else? Who was I just talking to? What is the date on the calendar – are we near a satanic festival?

A pattern of prayer/ministry for dealing with curses:

1) Submit our lives to the Lord.
2) Accept the love of God.
3) Pray for protection for loved ones and ourselves.
4) Pray for discernment, and wait on the Lord.
5) Break the curse (known by its effect on us) in the name of the Father, the Son and the Holy Spirit.
6) Break the psychic and spiritual links with the person who placed the curse. This is done simply in the name of Christ. For example, the prayer could be, 'In the name of Christ I break the psychic and spiritual links with x or y.'
7) Pray for a refilling of the Holy Spirit.

Resources that can be useful

Any resource that raises my awareness of my own state and of what God is saying is potentially useful. I have found of particular benefit very simple types of meditation. Simply sitting quietly and breathing in the love of God, exhaling fear, I have found enables me to be quiet and listen to God.

In Ignatian spirituality, the examen is a key component part of prayer that is normally carried out twice a day. Of particular note in the examen is the attention paid to emotion. This is of particular value in this area of ministry, as it is predominantly around the emotions that cursing has an effect. As a tool for prayer and awareness the examen is excellent.

The prayer of examen has two components. Firstly, it is looking at the day and seeing where God has been present to us, and how we have responded to His loving presence. Secondly, it is inviting the Lord to search our hearts to our deepest depths. As a prayer discipline it raises our awareness both of God and His love, and ourselves. For a brief introduction, Richard Foster's book *Prayer*[13] is excellent. For a more in-depth look at Ignatian spirituality, Larry Warner's book *Discovering the Spiritual Exercises of Saint Ignatius*[14] is very accessible.

[13] Richard Foster, *Prayer* (London: Hodder & Stoughton, 1992).
[14] Larry Warner, *Discovering the Spiritual Exercises of Saint Ignatius* (Oxford: BRF, 2011).

Chapter 6
Healing the History of the Community

Recently I was standing at the door of the church in Blurton waiting to take a wedding. I couldn't help overhearing a conversation which was taking place between three guests. All three were in their mid-twenties and were pushing prams up the church path.

'I had my chance to get out of here, but now it is too late,' said one of them. It felt like a cry of despair.

In the parish where I am vicar, we have three housing estates. These estates were originally built to house those who had work in the pottery industry and the coal mines. Stoke-on-Trent was world famous for the pottery industry, with such companies as Wedgwood, Moorcroft, Churchill, and many others. However, in recent times a lot of manufacturing has been outsourced abroad, and the subsequent decline of industry in the Potteries has had an immense impact on this community. All the coal mines have now closed, and there has been a loss of identity for the city. This, coupled with high unemployment, has led to a deep sense of rootlessness and despair. Robert Mountford in his book, *Heal the Land*,[15] details the history

---

[15] Robert Mountford, *Heal the Land* (Stoke-on-Trent: Tentmaker Press, 2011).

of Stoke-on-Trent, and he comments that because it was such a specialised manufacturing town, when the pottery industry declined there was no other heritage to fall back on.

When I first arrived at the parish of Blurton and Dresden, I will always remember going to St Alban's Church, in the middle of one of these three estates. It was positioned brilliantly, opposite the main shops of the community and next to the health centre. However, it was built in the late 1950s and the building was showing its age. As I was being shown around the church, I heard God say, 'This is where I will build my church.' Every Sunday a congregation of about a dozen faithful people worshipped here; all were elderly, and remembered how the church had flourished at its outset in the fifties. The other church in the parish, St Bartholomew's, grew rapidly, and it was decided to plant a new church in St Alban's. This we did, and over the next few years the new congregation became established. Different members of the congregation were involved in all aspects of the community, resident associations, and different social activities. Within St Alban's we had started a community café and a nursery.

In time, though, one issue became very clear, and that was the fact that for a good 30 years there had been little or no substantial investment in the community. For us, one of the key issues was the state of the building. We had leaks, poor heating, rotting window frames. How were we going to deal with it? Over the next three or so years, I had several attempts at trying to get the necessary funds to refurbish the building. However, each time I failed. Then about eight years ago, it was if God said, 'Now is the time', and a team came together that raised the funds. This, however, like most things, did not go entirely smoothly, and I remember at one particularly critical point being in despair and fear. It so happened on the evening of that day, there was a joint churches' prayer and worship meeting. As I sat listening to the worship, but not really engaging, I heard God say almost audibly, 'Give the building back to the community.' This was a shock to my system. I knew that practically at one level it could not happen – the Church of England does not give its buildings away! But the principle was clear: it was to be God's building, not ours; it was to be the community's building, not ours – and it certainly was not to be *my* building. I let go, and said, 'Lord, it is Yours, and theirs.' The next day we heard that a major donor had agreed to part-fund the project.

As part of raising the funds we had to research the area quite carefully, looking particularly at the potential demand and need for the new build. The new build was to be not just a church building, but a place for the community; it needed a café, rooms for activities, etc.

The research showed that the area was, according to the deprivation indices, not performing well as regards health, education and social factors. This was in common with most of Stoke-on-Trent, which in the Experian report of September 2001 was the worst place to live in England. The report ranked Stoke-on-Trent according to ten indices: retail activity, quality of schools, house prices, unemployment, rates, disposable income per household, number of cars, level of motor crime, household theft and density of population. Out of 376 towns and cities, Stoke-on-Trent came number 376. However, even within Stoke-on-Trent, our area was in the bottom 30 per cent, according to these indices. This was not news to us; we were well aware of the issues that surrounded us, but to see it confirmed statistically was sobering.

Eventually the rebuilding of St Alban's was under way; it took nine months to complete and opened officially in 2010. But as St Alban's was rebuilt, so something astonishing started to happen in the community. Inward investment suddenly flowed into our community; new shops, flats and a community centre were built. Even the secondary school was completely rebuilt. Something was happening that was of God. Visible signs were apparent that this community was of value. Healing of history was taking place; hope was rising. In 2013, Ed Silvoso ran a city-wide conference on the subject of 'Transformation'. His book[16] under the same title looks at the effect of transformation when it occurs in the marketplace. Here the emphasis is not buildings but business. How God wants to bring transformation to our communities is going to be different for every community, and the role of each individual church within that process is going to be different. What is really important, though, is to listen to God, and know what God is calling the Church to do to meet the needs and hurts of the community. This is a function of prayer, listening, discernment and knowing the history of the area. It is not a function of bright ideas, nor of doing projects because they are needed. It is doing the right thing at the right time, because God has called it into being. Too often projects are done, often buildings, less

---

[16] Ed Silvoso, *Transformation* (Ventura, CA: Regal Books, 2007).

because God says so, but more because we think they are needed.

However, the history of the community at Blurton was not going to be met totally by a building. If you go back to the original businesses of the potteries and the mines, they were historically not well paid, and very oppressive. Because the industries were so specialised, the communities were very non-mobile. The deep roots of oppression went back generations and had become part of the culture. This was seen mainly in the attitudes people could hold. There is a tendency to see everything as always bad, always negative: there is little hope of changing anything, so don't try. Even if you do try, you will never succeed. On the positive side, though, there is a deep sense of family, and community (though this is becoming less so). Unfortunately, this ongoing cycle – the lack of available work, low aspirations – all help to reinforce the view that you will never change anything and things will never improve, and I, as an individual, am powerless.

Recently we had the devastating Ebola outbreak in West Africa, and it was hitting all the news. I happened to go into a grocery shop to buy a newspaper, and as I was doing so the shop assistant said quite seriously to me, 'Well, we won't be here next month; that Ebola is going to hit us.' Fortunately, that was not right, but the presumption of ' disaster was in keeping with the culture of the area. In October 2015 the local city council decided to have a market once a week in front of St Alban's. This was a great idea, as market prices are generally cheaper, and with it being local to the estate, it was hoped that it would take off. It has not, but what was surprising was the comments of some – it would never succeed, it was always going to fail, to mention just two. Failure was being exalted, as success would be too challenging.

Walter Wink wrote his famous trilogy on the *Powers*,[17] in which he ascribes the 'powers' and 'principalities' (NKJV) as described by Paul in Ephesians 6, to the prevailing culture and history of an area. This, he says, has a real effect upon individuals and communities. I would without a doubt agree; if individuals can affect one another, if emotions and their energy can be experienced by another, then there is in my mind little doubt a community's emotional history and culture can have a wider effect. It is not easy to say how this is experienced. At one level it might just be the feel of a place when you come into it. Or potentially there are great effects – for example, the health statistics for the Blurton area leave much room for improvement.

This dynamic is a physical, emotional and spiritual one. In the 1990s, perhaps less so now, there was considerable emphasis on territorial spirits. This drew on the theology of Peter Wagner and others, where there was presumed to be a hierarchy of demons, perhaps seen in the list of Ephesians 6:12. I am not totally persuaded by this, but I am convinced by the reality that communities have a corporate dynamic that is often sinful, as it works against relationships with God and each other. In the main, I suspect that this does not need a demonic presence. Why have one if the job is already being done? However, if a community has a church within it that is bringing freedom,

---

17 Walter Wink, *Powers* (Minneapolis, MN: Augsburg Fortress, 1992).

healing and forgiveness, then the demonic may well be involved as the 'spirit of the area', feeding upon the sin of the place, and trying to hold it in position, by resisting the Church's efforts to bring that freedom. This places the local church firmly into the arena of spiritual warfare. To address this, though, the church needs to deal with both history and the demonic.

For the Church, the main weapons are worship and prayer. Worship in all its forms has an inbuilt dynamic: we are recognising the presence and nature of God, while acknowledging that He is Lord, and His agenda is what we want. This is the opening of the Lord's Prayer: 'Our Father in heaven, hallowed be your name, your kingdom come, your will be done, on earth as it is in heaven' (Matthew 6:9-10).

We are welcoming Him into our situation. We are meeting with Him, and you cannot meet with God and not be changed. But this is not just an individual or even a church dynamic. Because we bring the community into the church (because we are part of it), we are inviting the presence and grace of God to transform our communities; to forgive us our sin, to bring new hope and life. Every church has its own particular way of doing worship. For me, though, nowhere does this dynamic have a tighter focus than in the celebration of Holy Communion. Here the cross is held up for the community (indeed, for the world) and from the cross flows the river of life. Here, in the cross and resurrection, comes the definitive statement that evil will not triumph, sin has been forgiven, and relationship with God has been restored.

I remember talking to a Catholic priest, and his words still stick with me: 'When I celebrate the Eucharist, I do it for the community.'

The Church has the incredible, if slightly daunting, responsibility of bringing the community in all its facets to God. However, often the Church fails to realise that this is what it is doing! Church can so easily become a *personal* experience, even a *church* experience, not seeing that God wants a *community* experience. The cross was never just for the Church, but for the world. The reality is that God wants you and me to bring the kingdom of heaven into our communities; He wants to empower us to bring His presence into our workplace, into our homes, to families and friends. The years of history can only be addressed when they are brought into the saving presence of God, for forgiveness and healing. This means the Church as part of the community needs to own community history, and bring it to God. How this is done is for individual churches to decide. But it needs to be done. Within this process there may well be a demonic element that needs to be addressed. This has to be discerned through prayer, but the indicators of such a presence would be an internal resistance to prayer, unwillingness to engage, an increase in illness, relationships breaking down, etc. All of these would indicate an increase in demonic activity.

The process starts with prayer that leads to action. Recently in our church we did the *Fruitfulness on the Frontline* course,[18] which is all about seeing God at work wherever you are, 24/7. Rarely in my experience is

---

[18] Mark Greene, *Fruitfulness on the Frontline* (London: IVP, 2014).

transformation about the big things. More often than not, it is about loving your neighbour, praying for your street. At the core, though, are two things – firstly, my relationship with God, and secondly, my relationship with my brothers and sisters.

In each community, the history of that community is passed down, often from generation to generation. How the history is passed down is through memory. However, memory is multifaceted. In psychotherapeutic terms, memory has at least three different broad categories. There is cognitive memory: I remember what I had for breakfast. There is emotional memory, which is not cognitive, but is an emotional reaction that occurs when circumstances similar to the original event or pattern of events trigger the response. For example, being put down by another can easily produce anger that is out of proportion to the actual event, but is triggering the emotional response of years of being put down. And there is body memory, where the body reacts automatically to an event, because memory is stored in the muscles. For example, when someone has been badly physically abused when young, they may well instinctively curl up to protect themselves, and this then occurs later in life if they perceive they are under threat.

In community terms, we have cognitive memory. We know what happened when. We remember when the coal pit closed down, and we have a community experience of that. We have an emotional memory that is seen often in the emotional response of a community to perceived threat or injustice. For example, the miners' strike in the UK in 1984 carried deep emotions of injustice, among others. We have body memory where the memory is held in the actual physical land of the place. The idea that land can hold memory is well recognised biblically. In the Old Testament, the theology of place is important. The children of Israel often had to carry out quite brutal cleansing of communities. The high places with their altars to other gods had to be torn down. Places where God met His people were holy; places were named after experiences with God (for example, Genesis 22:14). In the New Testament, places of worship were important, and we have Jesus cleansing the Temple.

The Church is called to address all facets of memory. One of the ways this is done is by prayer-walking. This has a history in the Church with 'rogation' days, where the church members would walk around the parish (in Anglican terms), blessing the land and the crops. Prayer-walking can address all these memory types, but we have found that this is less a function of specific laid-down prayers (though that can be useful), but more of walking prayerfully through a place and listening to what God wants to deal with there. But perhaps more critical than this is the idea that it is the responsibility of every church member to bring God's presence into where they are now. This is done primarily by blessing: blessing places with God's peace, and blessing people with God's love.

Russ Parker in his book, *Rediscovering the Ministry of Blessing*, details this ministry. As he points out, blessing is rooted in the Old and New Testaments. Because it is the invoking of the love of God, he states that 'we must not lose sight of the nature of biblical blessing, which is the expectancy that in doing this we gain some tangible outcome from God'.[19] God wants to set free; He wants to bless.

---

[19] Russ Parker, *Rediscovering the Ministry of Blessing* (London: SPCK) p.20.

Chapter 7
Healing the Church

> For I am convinced that neither death nor life,
> neither angels nor demons, neither the present
> nor the future, nor any powers, neither height nor
> depth, nor anything else in all creation, will be
> able to separate us from the love of God that is in
> Christ Jesus our Lord.
> *Romans 8:38-39*

Memory holds the history of a community. That memory
is cognitive, emotional, and held in a physical
environment. Unless heard, validated and brought into the
presence of God, it will always repeat, and be a source of
sin (that which separates us from God and each other). The
demonic and Satan love that separation: that is their goal.

In the last chapter we looked at how the Church needs
to engage with the community to heal the community's
history. Because memory is held differently, the Church
will need to engage in different ways on different
occasions, as God leads. The efficacy of the Church,
though, is directly linked to its relationship with Christ, as
it is from this relationship that the Church derives its
authority and power. In this chapter we are looking at
what compromises the Church.

Firstly, the physical place of a church. For those of us privileged to worship in a building built centuries ago and enhanced, generation by generation, with loving care, the blessings can be considerable, but there are two major problems.

We can fall in love with the building and put it before the Lord and His priorities for the present generation. So we fall into idolatry. This, according to the Old Testament prophets, is unfaithfulness and puts us at odds with God. Anyone who is unable to worship anywhere else other than in the beautiful local church may well have fallen into this trap. 'We love the place, O God'[20] can be a dangerous hymn if our attention is focused on the love of the building, instead of love and reverence for the Lord. Satan loves idolatry since it deflects the worship from God, robs it of reality, and establishes another step along the way to drawing the worship to himself. He tried to persuade Jesus to engage in it in the wilderness, by tempting Him to bow down and worship him, and rule the kingdom without having to make the ultimate sacrifice (see Matthew 4:8-9).

Inevitably, any form of idolatry makes us vulnerable to demonic attack, should it come our way.

Also, the church may well have been built on an ancient pagan site. It was a deliberate strategy of our early forebears to build Christian churches and settlements on former occultic sites after consecrating the ground. While this was no doubt an admirable policy for them in their situation, it has stored up problems for our generation. The repeal of the Witchcraft Laws in 1951 in the UK sent signals

---

[20] William Bullock (1798–1874).

far and wide. It said to the nation that occult activity was now considered harmless, since one assumes that the government only legislates against things that are injurious to the general public. This has opened the floodgates to such activity in our day and brought about a proliferation of groups who operate with confidence since they are no longer illegal. They now turn their attention to the former occultic sites on which many ancient churches stand and try to revive the old powers. Those who worship Sunday by Sunday in such a building may sense the effects of such activity.

In our ministry across the 580 Anglican churches in the Lichfield diocese, we have found that the churches which experience the most problems in this area are those that are built on such sites. Occasionally they have been subject to occultic groups visiting the church building.

Sometimes this also applies to graveyards where there has been a burial of a person who was heavily involved in the occult.

One of the churches I minister in, St Bartholomew's, was built at least 500 years ago, although there may have been a church there prior to that. The church is built 50 yards away from a spring that has never to my knowledge run dry. While there is no direct evidence that the church was built on an ancient pagan site, it seems a reasonable conjecture. In the time that I have been vicar, and with my two predecessors, the primary issue that we faced in the church was conflict over worship. Consistently we have had to pray for those involved in worship and bless the land on which the church was built. To attribute this to the land is not far-fetched as the land has a deep history of pagan worship that would clash with worship of God.

Secondly, the emotional psychological history. Because all of us are human, we bring into the Church our own histories and hang-ups. Sometimes these prejudices (which are often based on fear) become collective and owned by the wider Church community. At the current time of writing, Europe is facing huge challenges over the immigration crisis. The collective fear is giving rise to tougher policies. Likewise, in the Church, fears can easily become collective, particularly if based on long-standing historical biases. Church leaders can sometimes find themselves overwhelmed by the collective history and fail to address it, or they may well find themselves on the receiving end of such history. For example, a church community can have an inbuilt hatred of authority, based on the history of being oppressed by authority, that is then expressed towards a church leader. This is unlikely to be open antagonism (though it can be!), but more often subtle and seen in the lack of movement of a church, and unwillingness to do what is necessary. Unless addressed, it will not matter how gifted the leader is, nothing will move. The effect of this on a leader can be devastating, giving rise to depression, health and family problems.

This can have consequences that are far-reaching. In the 1950s in our area, new estates were being built, particularly to house those working in the pottery and mining industry. The parish decided to build a church on the new estate that was only about 500 metres from the old church (St Bartholomew's). Plans were drawn up that included a parish hall as well as a church, but in the end only the church was built. The congregation at the time at St Bartholomew's was drawn from the owner-occupied houses in the area, and was seen as 'posh'. The church on the estate was to be built in part to keep those on the estate away from the main church – they could have St Alban's. It is not surprising that with this history, St Alban's struggled – it was seen as second best, and not quite good enough. We had to address this as a parish, through owning what happened, and going through the process of repentance. We found Russ Parker's book *Healing Wounded History* useful here. This was prior to St Alban's being rebuilt, but even so we find that critical attitudes can easily creep back, and from time to time we have to readdress the issue.

Thirdly, cognitive history. This is the history that we know, the issues that are live now and of which we are aware. We may well not want to recognise it, but it is there all the same. As mentioned in Chapter 5, the Church has seemed to avoid the inner journey. This is coming back now, with the increased interest in, for example, Ignatian and Celtic spirituality. But what are we avoiding? Going too deep? Not facing the challenges that we ought to? Could it be that the Church has made the Christian faith a consumer product, to take and leave, to make one feel good? It is essential that the Church has the courage to stop being avoidant. As a Church in the widest sense, we are sinful; this is unavoidable as we are human beings, but what is necessary is that the path of forgiveness, growing in holiness, and in relationship with God and each other, continues.

The area where we most clearly see corporate sin is with money. Henry Chadwick, in his book *The Early Church*, attributes the rapid growth of the early Church prior to Constantine to the incredible generosity and open-handedness of the churches:

> The practical application of charity was probably the most potent single cause of Christian success. The pagan comment 'See how these Christians love one another' (reported by Tertullian) was not irony. Christian charity expressed itself in care for the poor, for widows, and orphans, in visits to the brethren in prison or to those condemned to the living death of labour in the mines, and in social action in time of calamity like famine, earthquake, pestilence or war.[21]

All of those actions must have been very costly in time, goods and money. Today the Church of England as an institution is fighting for money. The number of people attending church has declined over the last ten years, the number of buildings has remained the same, the need for money is stark, to maintain the church, to keep the show on the road. Church ministers are placed under pressure to produce the goods. Those in charge of the organisation know that we are hanging on, just.

---

[21] Henry Chadwick, *The Early Church* (London: Penguin, 1993) p.56.

If you add to the mix the insecurity generated by the banking collapse from 2008 onwards, the cutbacks to services, as society can no longer afford them, the increasing price of housing, then you have an environment that easily generates fear. Am I going to have enough? Am I as a minister going to generate sufficient revenue for the institution, so I get paid? In this context charity, and giving, faces the fear of not having enough. It poses the question: whom do we serve – mammon or God? Where society tells me that my self-worth is tied to my wealth, what happens if I do not have enough?

It is not easy for the church or the individual to recognise their dependence on God; we talk about it, we know it, but do we live it? Or is the truth that we live in idolatry? Facing these questions, bringing them before God, acknowledging the issues is critical. It will mean living in vulnerability, depending on God, but failure to do so means that we are very vulnerable to demonic attack.

Of course there are churches that are marvellous examples of God's generosity and love. Yet there are not many. 'Open-handedness' is not one of our renowned characteristics. It seems that we are ensnared by corporate sin; we are bound up in the world's values.

Idolatry

Usually when Christians consider the issue of idolatry, a number of things are trotted out, such as money and materialism, having a good time. But there is another subtle form of idolatry. There is little doubt that the continuing collapse in the nuclear and extended family is having a major impact on the mental health of our nation.

For mental health professionals, this is predominantly focused around the attachment and separation with the primary caregiver. The more dysfunctional the relationship between mother (normally) and child, the greater the likelihood of mental health problems in the future. For those coming to faith, the church becomes a safe place and that is excellent. Healing starts with safety.

However, as we have seen, Jesus gave both support and challenge, and this was within the context of bringing in the kingdom of God. For the Church it is the same. The danger is that because challenge is uncomfortable we dodge it, or use it as a mechanism to preserve the status quo. We can easily challenge others, because they do not think like us and therefore are a threat. Likewise, we can avoid the challenges to ourselves because they are too painful. In both of these cases the idol that is created almost unwittingly is the big I. The worship must be to my liking. A good service is one that meets my emotional needs, that makes me feel good. The big danger that the church then faces is that we lose our context, that of bringing the kingdom of God in to our society. The healing and wholeness that God brings is always in the context of the kingdom of God.

We meet together as the body of Christ, the Church, to worship. To meet with the risen Lord. Meeting with God means change, moving on. Psychotherapists use the idea of 'contact', whereby genuine meeting with another facilitates change. This I have seen time and time again. In genuine meeting, courage and hope rise to face the reality of what one did not have, to come to terms with the historical gaps, so they become history and choice, and do not dictate the present. Of course it takes time for fears to settle, and the process can be long and painful. But in the Church, if we genuinely facilitate the meeting of people with God and each other, what healing flows!

When we turn to the national scene, we see that the idolatry of the Church has had devastating consequences throughout the centuries, and has allowed the spread of the demonic on a huge scale.

John Dawson, in his book, *Taking Our Cities for God*, has this to say:

> In human history it is easy to see the enemy coming in like a flood and the Lord raising up a standard against him. In a global sense, each generation faces Satan in the form of the spirit of antichrist or world domination. This is the spirit behind those who have ambition to rule the world, such as Napoleon or Hitler ... a praying church should face this spirit and drive it off long before we find ourselves in a world at war. Physical violence represents an encroachment of spiritual violence into the material realm. The spirit of world domination can emerge only when the saints have lost their vigilance or when the international church has become severely divided over some issue.[22]

If one looks at the history of the Church in Germany prior to 1940, one can see how it had fallen into idolatry or 'lost its vigilance', as Dawson would put it. The success of

---

[22] John Dawson, *Taking Our Cities for God* (Lake Mary, FL: Charisma House, 1991) p.150.

National Socialism and the election of Adolf Hitler was welcomed by many in the churches. The 1920s had seen a rise in decadence and corruption, due to economic collapse, and had scandalised church leaders of all traditions.

After Hitler's Reichstag speech in March 1933, it was only a few months before a truce was signed between the Vatican and Hitler.

John Bowden in his book, *Karl Barth*, summarises the state of the German Church:

> From 1920s onwards, groups of German Protestant pastors, who tended on the whole to be politically conservative, patriotic and paternalistic, had been binding themselves into associations aimed at giving a purely German characteristic to the Christian Gospel. 'For a German' one of the milder statements goes, 'the Church is the community of believers who are obligated to fight for a Christian Germany.'

Another statement indicates which of the last two words is meant to bear the main stress: 'A godless fellow countryman is nearer to us than one of another race, even if he sings the same hymn or prays the same prayer.'[23]

These groups of pastors rapidly became united, with an eventual national bishop approved by Hitler. This was, however, opposed by other groups in the Church (Bonhoeffer and Neimöller among them), which eventually became the 'Confessing Church'.

---

[23] John Bowden, *Karl Barth* (London: SCM Press) pp.56,57.

Barth's comment was: 'In the last resort I saw my dear German people beginning to worship a false God.'[24] The reasons for the idolatry were probably rooted in the pain of the 1920s; the saviour was seen as Hitler, not Jesus Christ. If Dawson is right, the idolatry of the Church led to the appearance and power of Hitler, and the subsequent tragedy that engulfed the Jews and the whole world.

The failure of both the German Church up to 1940 (and the Dutch Reformed Church in its early years in South Africa) to be Christ-centred resulted in the nation and the Church falling into idolatry. This in turn allowed full play to the anger and hurt of humankind coupled with the demonic powers, with the suffering and chaos of which we are only too aware.

This is, of course, the basic pattern that we see particularly in the Old Testament. God is adapted to meet the needs of the people and idolatry results, with deadly consequences.

This is seen today at its most stark at a national level, but it is also seen at the local church level. The telltale signs include the lack of relevance of the Church to the community, the double standards concerning money, the lack of charity, an overblown sense of its own importance, and a dramatic increase in people being caught up in the demonic.

How does the Church deal with this? Just standing up and preaching it will not necessarily get you very far, as idolatry is rooted in the very being and fibre of most of us! In 2001 the situation in Stoke-on-Trent was not good, and

---

[24] Bowden, *Karl Barth*, p.57.

the church leaders met to pray with 2 Chronicles 7:14 as the focus: 'if my people, who are called by my name, will humble themselves and pray and seek my face and turn from their wicked ways, then I will hear from heaven, and I will forgive their sin and will heal their land.' This was the key verse, that was seen as necessary for the healing of Stoke-on-Trent.

Central to this was the recognition that it starts with leaders. Those whom God has called forward to lead His church take responsibility for the church.

The ACE principle: Awareness, Compassion, Engagement

Central to any movement forward, be it for an individual, a church or a city, is awareness of the problem. This is not as straightforward as it seems, as you can see an issue, but not necessarily own it for yourself! To own it for oneself needs courage, support and love. The church leaders in Stoke-on-Trent were not easily going to own their own failings, and the failings of their churches. Implicit in 2 Chronicles 7:14 is the knowledge of what you have done and what needs to change. This can take a considerable period of time, and the subsequent meetings of church leaders increased depths of openness and acceptance. Fears of competiveness were reduced, and support grew. It was this support that allowed a growing awareness of where the Church in the city was. For an individual church, this rests with the leadership as a whole.

As we have seen, central to Christ's engagement with us is compassion. This is what we need to give to each other, and receive from God. Judgement outside of acceptance and compassion is just condemnation, and goes nowhere. Being prepared to walk with each other is key. That is what we are committed to. This commitment flows not from ourselves, but the centrality of Christ, and His total commitment to us.

It is only when the awareness and compassion is in process that engagement can take place. The engagement happens at three levels: firstly with Christ, secondly with each other, and only then with the issue of idolatry (or the key presenting issue God is bringing up at the time). It is at this point that discernment will be needed to deal with the demonic. This may well involve praying about history, dealing with memory, etc.

Chapter 8
The Occult

As we saw in Chapter 3, the power of the demonic is always subject to God, and can have a number of effects. How the demonic interacts with human beings is important, as it determines how we deal with it. This is not just a function of getting rid of the demonic, but dealing with the issue of sin.

In the Old Testament, in Genesis 17 we see the covenant made by God with Abraham. It is 'an everlasting covenant' (v.7) made with Abraham and all his descendants, yet we need to note it is not an unconditional covenant. It is based on obedience (v.10). When the people are disobedient they open themselves to destruction.

In Exodus 32 the Israelites have made a golden calf, and the consequence of that disobedience is horrific – 3,000 people were killed (v.28). So despite the covenant being an everlasting covenant, it was not a licence to do what you please; the rebels were punished. The only way back was by repentance.

When we look at the New Testament, the principles of the covenant have not changed: we have been forgiven our sins because of Christ's death on the cross, we are new creations (as Paul says in 2 Corinthians 5:17), and we are not under law but under grace. As the covenant with

Abraham was based on faith, so for us it is based on relationship and faith in Christ:

> For God so loved the world that he gave his one and only Son, that whoever believes in him shall not perish but have eternal life.
> *John 3:16*

Even so, within this new everlasting covenant, rebellion has its consequences as it did for the children of Israel:

> If we claim to be without sin, we deceive ourselves and the truth is not in us. If we confess our sins, he is faithful and just and will forgive us our sins and purify us from all unrighteousness. If we claim we have not sinned, we make him out to be a liar and his word has no place in our lives.
> *1 John 1:8-10 (NIV 1984)*

To be under grace, and to know the loving protection of God, we need to be open and honest in our relationship with Him. We have to recognise rebellion for what it is and confess it. If we fail to do so 'his word has no place in our lives', and God may well allow us to be vulnerable to curses and the demonic so that we see our sin and repent.

Now, it is a fact that we are all saints who sin, and we will never be entirely free from sin until we reach heaven, and therefore we will be continually asking for God's forgiveness, grace and protection. Indeed, that is the message of the prayer Jesus taught us:

> This, then, is how you should pray:
> 'Our Father in heaven,

hallowed be your name,
your kingdom come,
your will be done,
on earth as it is in heaven.
Give us today our daily bread.
And forgive us our debts,
as we also have forgiven our debtors.
And lead us not into temptation,
but deliver us from the evil one.'
For if you forgive other people when they sin
against you, your heavenly Father will also
forgive you. But if you do not forgive others their
sins, your Father will not forgive your sins.
Matthew 6:9-15

Our sin is not just what we decide to do wrong, but is also a complex function of our upbringing and culture. All these factors can result in patterns of behaviour that are sinful because they act against relationships. But God expects us to be forgiving, as He is, because we know the incredible non-judgemental love of God. But the process of forgiveness is rarely straightforward.

It makes sense, then, that if there are areas in our lives that are constantly sinful (working against relationships), we will be vulnerable in these areas. Awareness which allows for confession is key, and this is often raised by curses and the demonic. Likewise, awareness of the presence and grace of God is also critical, because as it is pointed out in 1 Peter 4:8: 'Above all, love each other deeply, because love covers over a multitude of sins.' God knows that we are not perfect, but He does expect us to be in relationship with Him and work it through with Him and each other.

So when we are asked to help those who have been involved in occultic activities, we are doing so from the viewpoint that we are all saints who sin, but we know someone who can help! For God, people come first, His love is for us – and so it is when dealing with those who need help in this area.

The Occult

Occult means hidden and is applied to all sorts of activities that have a spiritual element to them. These can range from Yoga, fortune telling, Ouija boards, spiritualism and various forms of meditation, to psychic fairs, Satanism and witchcraft, to mention just a few. Why do people get involved with these activities? People get involved to meet a need they perceive in themselves.[25] In other words, it makes me feel good, it makes me feel relaxed, it makes me feel powerful, or whatever.

From a Christian perspective, it is much the same when people come to faith. They come to meet a need; they realise they are loved by God and He wants to meet them. Given that a very large percentage of the world's population have a faith of some variety, the need for faith would seem to be part of being human. What separates out the Christian faith is the character and nature of God. God as love, God as committed to you and me, God wanting to

---

[25] Some might also be true spiritual seekers who have rejected the established Church, or those who have been bereaved and are looking for 'proof' of an afterlife.

be in relationship with us. There are, of course, elements of that in other faiths, but nowhere except in the Christian faith does this have such a tight and personal focus.

From a Christian perspective, the key area of sin is idolatry. In the Old Testament, in Deuteronomy 7 it is clear that there is to be a driving out of the other nations from the land, their gods are to be destroyed and there is to be no intermarriage, because 'you are a people holy to the LORD your God' (v.6). Now, however difficult it is to live with the violence that is advocated, the principle is still clear. This is also seen with Jesus, and the cleansing of the Temple:

> Jesus entered the temple courts and drove out all who were buying and selling there. He overturned the tables of the money-changers and the benches of those selling doves. 'It is written,' he said to them, '"My house will be called a house of prayer," but you are making it "a den of robbers."'
> *Matthew 21:12-13*

Jesus is cleansing the Temple from the idolatry of money.

There are areas of the occult where idolatry is focused very deliberately on the demonic – for example, in Satanism. But it is obviously there in other areas as well, as the focus is not on God but on other gods or vague powers.

One of the most common forms of involvement that I have come across is Ouija boards. These are widely available and are sold as a game on the internet. Clearly, at times the pointer on the board (whatever form it takes) is moved subconsciously by the participants, but equally so there are times when it is not. I have had many instances of dealing with individuals who have come for help after using a Ouija board.

The issue about involvement with the occult is the aspect of choice. The individual consciously decides to engage in, for example, a séance. It is this conscious decision that is a deliberate act of sin that potentially exposes the individual to the demonic. It is a bit like walking across a busy road, blindfolded; you may not get hit, but the odds are, you will.

One of the issues in Western society is, because of the rise of individualism and consumerism, it is seen as perfectly valid to take bits from various faiths and use them to meet our own needs for peace and well-being. Every faith operates within a framework that is much larger than its individual forms of practice. For example, you cannot isolate the Lord's Prayer from the nature of God. Indeed, if you do take things out of their overall context it can be dangerous, as the sons of Sceva found out in Acts 19:13-16. But this is what has been done particularly in the areas of Yoga and mindfulness. Yoga can be associated with Hinduism, and mindfulness can be associated with Buddhism. Both of these practices can be extremely beneficial, but they belong within the context of these faiths. All faiths have an awareness of the demonic, and evil, and claim to have evolved ways of staying safe.

Dr Dingwall-Jones, writing in the *Church Times* (24th March 2016), highlights this, particularly in regard to mindfulness. He draws attention to a study in the University of California where 63 per cent of those who were involved in meditation had experienced negative effects such as anxiety, depression, sobbing and mild dissociation. He rightly points out that the Christian mystical tradition (for example, St John of the Cross in the `Dark Night of the Soul') has a lot of wisdom to offer in this area. Jesus was very aware of living in the present and being mindful. For example, we see in Matthew 6:25-34: 'Therefore do not worry about tomorrow' (v.34), and how to do this is clear: 'seek first his kingdom and his righteousness' (v.33).

This is not to say that one cannot learn from different faith practices, but it is to say that they belong within the overall context of the faith to which they are taken from. Different faiths contain different forms of wisdom, and can learn and assimilate from one another. But what is important is to realise that these are not techniques to make me feel better, but genuine spiritual practices that are rooted within a defined spiritual framework. It is not enough for the Christian to unthinkingly assimilate them; as Jesus said in John 14:6, He is the way, the truth and the life, and no one comes to the Father except through Him. There is an arrogance, or perhaps ignorance, to think that I can use these practices for my own gratification, with no spiritual consequences. Again the sin of idolatry raises its head.

Satanism, though, is the deliberate worship of the very body that is anti-God, and it is very clear that this is demonic. Satanism has various denominations, much like the Church. Within satanic denominations there are different emphases, but perhaps the most committed are the groups where membership is passed down from generation to generation. Survivors' reports of ritual satanic abuse make shocking reading. But what is perhaps more shocking are the consistent attempts to ridicule the reports and write them off as hysterical. Those groups involved in the therapy of those who have been abused in this way know the truth of these reports.

How to deal with occultic involvement

In the Church of England, we have a system of child baptism, followed by confirmation at a later date, normally these days when one is an adult. In the baptism service there is a specific prayer for deliverance used by the minister:

> May almighty God deliver you from the powers
> of darkness, restore in you the image of his glory,
> and lead you in the light and obedience of Christ.
> Amen.[26]

This, however, is extremely low-key compared to some of the Greek Orthodox liturgies, which probably reflects more accurately the tradition of the early Church, where deliverance was a long process prior to the actual baptism. In the Anglican system, confirmation is the confirming of the baptism vows, and the public declaration of faith. I remember one year asking the adult candidates how many of them had been involved in the past with either Ouija boards, spiritualism, etc. Out of 12, 11 had some

---

[26] *Common Worship: Services and Prayers for the Church of England* (London: Church House Publishing, 2000), p.354.

experience. This was mainly Ouija boards and fortune tellers. For most it was a bit of fun, but one had found it frightening.

To realise what they had willingly done was quite a shock. But the process of dealing with it was relatively straightforward:

1) The individuals needed to acknowledge before God that they had sinned (confession). This was not just a function of realising that they had done something wrong, but also acknowledging the sin of idolatry behind what they did. They put themselves first.

2) They needed to ask for God's forgiveness.

3) They received God's forgiveness, through the words of absolution.

4) They asked God to pour out His Holy Spirit on them anew.

This was done in small groups, and passed off relatively quietly. But this is not always the case. On one occasion a person refused to confess, and got quite agitated. After talking gently, he calmed down, but still could not confess. It was not that he didn't want to but the words would simply not come out. Along with another senior church member we together sensed that there was a demon there, and so we, in the name of Christ, commanded the demon of the Ouija board to depart into the hands of Christ. Immediately he could speak and confess. It was particularly important to pray the Holy Spirit on him afresh, so that he knew God's love and protection surrounding him.

In the case of a demon being present we follow what Jesus did with the Gerasenes swine (Luke 8:32); He sent the demons into the pigs. I take the view that Jesus is by far the safest place for demons to be, so send them into the hands of Christ. With all deliverance ministry I try to keep it as low-key as possible, and as matter-of-fact as I can. It is traumatic enough already, and shouting only adds to it. There is another reason, though, for placing evil spirits/demons into the hands of Christ, and this is found in Luke:

> When an impure spirit comes out of a person, it goes through arid places seeking rest and does not find it. Then it says, 'I will return to the house I left.' When it arrives, it finds the house swept clean and put in order. Then it goes and takes seven other spirits more wicked than itself, and they go in and live there. And the final condition of that person is worse than the first.
> *Luke 11:24-26*

The idea of an evil spirit just wandering around is clearly not very good news from this passage. In this ministry we move in the safety and authority of Christ, so He can hold them. Likewise, the idea that the demons can come back is disturbing, so as a matter of course we always pray for the infilling of the Holy Spirit at the end. Finally, after the time of prayer we would also be asking the question: Is there an underlying pastoral issue that needs to be addressed here? Why did this person get involved?

What was it that made him or her vulnerable? This we would ask the person to explore either with ourselves or with a member of the pastoral team. God always wants to bring healing and wholeness.

Certain organisations use checklists with people to see if there is any possibility of demonic oppression.[27] These certainly have their place within the context of a ministering community. There is little doubt that more and more people have had contact with the occult, and I wonder whether, if we were more rigorous in this area, we would avoid a lot of problems.

The practical guidelines that we use in our church ministry are as follows:

1) Enthrone God – not the 'principalities and powers' (Deuteronomy 20:1-4).

2) We minister from the victory of Christ, we do not fight for a victory (Colossians 2:15).

3) Rely upon God's active help: God's Word, His authority (Luke 9:1ff), His gifts (1 Corinthians 12).

4) Do not let the devil set the agenda, nor the time, nor the type of ministry. Buy time by 'binding' if necessary. At the same time signal to the person coming for prayer that they are being taken seriously. A binding prayer simply binds all the powers of evil, and commands them in the name of Christ not to cause any harm. Often I have been approached at a time

---

[27] For example, http://www.christianhealingmin.org – look at the forms section (accessed 21st October 2016).

when the deliverance ministry was not advisable (a lack of privacy, or prayer support was not present), so I have used such a prayer, and set up a more appropriate time.

5) Work in teams. This helps avoids spiritual pride, and false accusation.

6) Do not overreact – most people coming to faith today have been involved in some occult. Not all unexplainable phenomena are of the devil! Avoid using terms such as 'possession' and 'exorcism'. These are very emotive terms that can cause a fear reaction. Be aware that mental illness can produce very bizarre behaviour.

7) Deliverance is into Jesus as well as from evil. Repentance, the owning of wrongdoing, saying sorry, and being prepared to turn to Christ, is critical for the individual to come to wholeness. Long-term pastoral care, rather than just short-term ministry, should be our aim, and this is the responsibility of the church, under the guidance of deliverance team members where necessary.

8) Realise that there are degrees of influence. Much is fairly minor, but occasionally we encounter more serious manifestations where the victim is no longer free to be the person God wants them to be.

Timing is one of the key areas here. Many a time my phone has rung at night with someone asking for the deliverance ministry. Set the time and the place. I always use the church, not my home, and always work in a team. Often I will ask for prayer support as necessary.

Occasionally we come across Satanists who have been sent into churches to cause splits and destruction by cursing. If you think that such a person is in your congregation, then by far the best thing to do is to set a team on blessing them in prayer. We have had situations where it has then transpired that the individual wants to come out of the satanic group that sent them. At one level this is a tremendous compliment, both that you are under such attack, and more importantly that the love of Christ has reached out to that person. What needs to then happen is the involvement of other agencies. This could be the police, social services, and specialised counselling agencies. The level of psychological damage that the individual may have sustained as a result of being in the cult is enormous. Often this can result in dissociative disorders that can seem very bizarre, such as speaking in different voices. It is important that no deliverance ministry takes place at this time, as it can easily increase the level of psychological damage. What is needed is pastoral support and care, with other agencies dealing with the wounds that have occurred. The pastoral care needs to be clearly defined: who is responsible for what and when, as the demands can be very high. Ideally it will not involve church leaders. The danger of not doing this has been seen time and time again over the years, with ministers having to leave their ministry because they became too involved, and didn't realise their own limitations.

It can be a very long journey to come out of a cult, and it may need the person to be relocated.

Chapter 9
Natural Phenomena and Dealing with Buildings

Psychic abilities

A number of years ago I went with John Widdas to see an organisation that was helping those who wanted to come out of cults, particularly Satanism. As part of the visit we had agreed to meet a couple of those who were coming out, as well as those helping them. One person came into the room, took one look at me and said, 'You're psychic, aren't you?'

The word 'psychic' is now much misunderstood, partly because of its commercialisation – people go to psychics to see the future, receive reassurance, etc. My personal experience involved being very sensitive to other people's emotions, picking them up very easily and sometimes not understanding what was going on, just feeling overwhelmed. Occasionally I knew exactly what people were thinking, and I often had dreams about places that I would visit at a later date. I would get a sense of foreboding if something unpleasant was about to happen either to myself or to others. From time to time I would know exactly what someone was doing, even if it was at a great distance. To be honest, I never paid these things a great deal of attention, because this was normal for me, until a situation arose when I was involved in praying for someone.

The person concerned had been involved in all sorts of situations that had caused a great deal of pain. When two or three of us were praying, I suddenly knew what had happened to him, and thought that was what God wanted me to pray for. So I did, but the results were not good. What I knew was not a word of knowledge from God, as the effect, if it had been, would have been positive. Neither was it a spirit of divination as in Acts 16, as it was not concerned with the future. It threw the person concerned into trauma that then needed others much more skilled than I to help him through. I decided then that being 'psychic' was not necessarily good news or a gift. The other side of it was that it was exhausting and not a little unnerving. In talking to others who were equally sensitive, this was a common experience. One was terrified as she often had dreams of accidents that then happened. She thought she was causing them.

The reason why one person is 'psychic' and another isn't is unknown. But it does tend to run in families. This may simply be a function of normal human dynamics where familiar traits are passed down from generation to generation. This is not be confused with familiar spirits. Familiar spirits are referred to in spiritualism and seen in different cultures, for example in shamanism, and in parts of Finnish culture. The experience of familiar spirits is of something external to oneself, a presence that informs and is in some cases believed to protect. This is not the experience of someone who is psychic. The psychic just happens; it arises not from another being, but from an internal experience. The experience of channeling a spirit, as seen in séances, is at the deliberate and conscious invitation of the medium; this is not psychic. But those who are psychic often get involved in spiritualism, new age activities, or the Church. It may just be an enhanced ability to process emotional information; it may be a human ability that we have when very young, but most grow out of as verbal skills increase. But whatever the reason, it is there. One of the people we met who was coming out of Satanism described being psychic in this way: 'the capacity to wander over the spiritual plain'.

My personal view of the psychic is that this ability is due to developmental problems that can arise between the main caregiver and the child. Many mothers just know their young baby needs feeding, or changing; they don't need the child to tell them. Somehow they are just picking up the unspoken needs – somehow the child is telling the mother what he or she needs. Normally, most human beings grow out of this way of communicating, but some do not. They retain this capacity to communicate and receive communication and information without words. The ability is retained because this is what the child needs to be safe. This is not so wild a supposition as it first seems; the more quantum physics is developed, the more we realise that we actually interact with each other not just on verbal or physical levels, but by the interchange of all sorts of particles. Being psychic has emotional, spiritual and physical dimensions, but is, as far as I can see, a human condition that some have in the same way that some are born with artistic abilities.

However, unlike artistic abilities, which are a positive attribute, being psychic rarely is, because of the profound emotional and spiritual dynamics. As I discovered to my cost, knowing psychically is not the same as knowing what God wants to do at any one time. It is, however, addictive; it is an ability that is with one from a very early age (I remember, for example, instances from the age of five). It can give the sense of being special, and keeping one safe. So there can be a reluctance to let go of this ability, and once one has, there can be a temptation under pressure to return to it.

For the Christian, safety is with God, in His love and grace, moving where He directs. This is not the same as knowing psychically. It is very different, as the point of reference is always God, not what I have picked up or know. So how do we minister to those who come for help in this area?

1) Recognise that it takes a great deal of courage for someone to seek God's healing, as it is an ability that is deeply embedded within a person.

2) This is rarely a quick-fix prayer and often needs ongoing awareness and bringing to God. Because it is a natural ability, what is needed is choice, and the person being ministered to has to realise that God is giving them the power to choose not to use the psychic. In my experience, it does not just disappear.

3) One of the concepts that I have found it helpful to understand in this area is that of the third eye. The

third eye comes from occultic and Hindu roots, where, on the forehead is the eye that sees and perceives beyond normal perception.

When someone comes for ministry in this area, I ask them:

1) To tell God that they want to lay this down and have their security in Him and that they only want to see what God is telling and showing them.

2) To confess to God that they have used this ability for their own security and sometimes gain.

After they have done this I make the sign of the cross on their forehead with oil (that has been blessed for the healing ministry), and simply say: 'In the name of the Father, and of the Son, and of the Holy Spirit, I close your third eye.'

This is a prayer that the person has to use for themselves: almost on a daily basis to begin with, as it is so tempting, almost automatic to go back to the psychic. What also helps is to suggest a discipline of prayer. The psychic by its nature is very undisciplined, so a framework of daily prayer and Bible study is very useful.

Psychics easily pick up both other people's feelings, carrying their emotions, and also the demonic. If the demonic is around, one of the key features will be to resist all prayer at closing down this ability. Sometimes it is also required that they put down the people's feelings they are carrying, and entrust them to God's safe-keeping.

Occasionally I have come across churches that have someone who is psychic on their prayer team. This is not good news, as psychic knowledge is not a 'word of knowledge' as given by God, as I found out. Anyone who is on a prayer team must have sorted this out before praying for anyone else!

Poltergeists

This is an area that has been massively glamorised in films. All definitions on the web that I have found say that a poltergeist is a ghost or supernatural being that throws things around. I don't believe that this is true in the main; in my experience, the majority of such cases are due to unresolved or avoided trauma. If you avoid trauma, you avoid the emotional energy that goes with it, and so the energy has to go somewhere else. In most cases this can mean turning it in on oneself, giving increased fear and anxiety, or even occasionally physical symptoms, such as stomach upsets. Sometimes, though, that energy and force is expressed through the disruptions of objects, or electrics, and it is this that is categorised as poltergeist activity.

I was called to a house where the owner of the house was a plumber, and he was extremely embarrassed and upset. For some reason water had been collecting in pools in different rooms of the house, and this had been going on for about six weeks. In those six weeks he had ripped up most of the floorboards, and checked most of the pipe joints. When I arrived the house still looked as though a bomb had hit it. However, the water was still appearing despite all the plumbing being OK. The Church was his last resort. As we sat down and talked, a sad and desperate story emerged. He has lost his wife to cancer; she had died about three months before. They had three children, the eldest of whom was a girl of 17. She was now running the house, making sure everyone got off to school, dealing with the washing, and doing the household chores. We talked both to him and to the eldest child. In talking to the eldest child, it was clear that she had had no time to grieve the loss of her mother. Suitable counselling was arranged for her. When the counselling started, the water stopped appearing. Her unresolved grief was expressing itself through the appearance of the water. Why water? Well, this may have been the way her subconscious was calling for help from her father as, of course, he was a plumber.

On numerous occasions we have dealt with cases that have involved electrics turning on and off, pictures coming off walls, items disappearing and reappearing (and not just because of faulty memory!). Other areas of repressed trauma have included those suffering from depression, and anger issues. The mechanism by which this happens is not clearly understood.

It is tempting for the Christian minister to treat poltergeist activity like the demonic, as the symptoms seem bizarre and frightening, and often those who suffer from this activity believe it to be demonic. But one has to ask the question, why would the demonic do this? What is to be gained by it? There are certainly no references to this kind of activity in the Bible. I suspect that the strange manifestations are not to do with the demonic but much more to do with disturbed human beings.

However, what may well be true is that members of the house have been involved in occultic activity, such as playing on a Ouija board, using Tarot cards, or being involved in séances. In this case, because the demonic has effectively been given permission by the person or persons involved, it may well be present in the individuals or the house. The presence of the demonic may have the effect of increasing the repression of emotion that then causes the poltergeist activity. Deliverance then will have an immediate effect, as the demonic is released from the person, and the emotions may well then be expressed and heard.

So when dealing with poltergeist activity, ask first whether there has been any occultic activity, and prayerfully deal with it, before going on to enquire about the psychological aspects. Repressed memories are repressed for a reason, normally because they are too painful to face, so great gentleness and empathy is needed, and it may well take several sessions. Shame and guilt are common here, and prayers for peace and the knowledge of the unconditional love of God are very effective. It is a wonderful opportunity for sharing the love of Christ.

With repressed memory, we need to understand that the repression is a way of survival, so it does no good to try to 'break through' the repression, as this simply raises more fear. Gently affirming the repression is much more effective at releasing the memory and emotion, as fear is reduced. Saying something like, 'It is OK not to say; I understand it is too painful', can be much more freeing than saying, 'Try to tell me.' The first statement is affirming and so reduces the fear, the second is challenging and therefore increases the fear.

Because poltergeist activity is memory-based, it is always worth asking when the events started happening. Memory needs a trigger to become active. Bad memories that have been repressed can be triggered by news items, or trauma. Emotional repression is commonly found in the teenage years. Teenage years are the time when you are finding your identity and independence. This can act as a trigger for the very early memories of attachment and separation when one was young, typically around 12 to 24 months old. If these emotional memories were not good, they can give rise to deep feelings of rejection and worthlessness that are ignored or repressed. It is very unlikely that these will be recalled memories of actual events; they are much more likely to be feelings, or emotional memories as opposed to cognitive ones.

Dealing with buildings

One of the most common reasons that we find people approaching the Church is problems in their homes. There is something wrong in their house. Something doesn't feel right, the children will not sleep, footsteps are heard on the stairs, figures are seen.

Generally, these fall into the following categories;

1) **Place Memory.** In this scenario, the same ghostly 'picture' appears to some people. Always in the same place, and always repeating the same action. Pray for peace in the house, reassure them that if they see the apparition again it will do nothing, and cause no harm. It is not a ghost! It is almost as if the fabric of the place has absorbed the memory.

2) **'Unquiet Dead'** – 'Appearances'. This can be more disturbing and sometimes quite frightening. Figures of people are seen in places and move around. Often children will report someone at the end of the bed. Pets can get very disturbed and refuse to go into certain areas of the house. There can be places in the house that feel abnormally cold.

3) **Occultic activity has taken place/is taking place in a house.** This can result in all sorts of phenomena, including poltergeist-like activity, banging, etc.

4) **The Land.** Sometimes the land a place is built on carries its own memories that have been disturbed. This can then affect those in the house.

Blessing a house and asking for God's presence will remove place memory.

The 'unquiet dead' is a category that does not easily fit with biblical theology. One explanation is that what you are actually dealing with is a familiar spirit masquerading as a dead person. This may well be the case, particularly when there has been a medium involved, or the appearances started after, say, a Ouija board session. In part this can explain Leviticus 19:31: 'Do not turn to mediums or seek out spiritists, for you will be defiled by them. I am the LORD your God.' What is actually being called up is a demonic spirit, and that is genuinely defiling. If this is the case, one of the first questions that needs to be asked in the house is: 'Have you had a medium in here, been to a spiritualist church, or been involved in the occult in any way?' If occultic activity is taking place in a house, then it must be made clear to the occupants that this must stop, and there needs to be confession, repentance, forgiveness and appropriate ministry. This necessitates turning to Christ as Lord, as the space left by the demonic must be filled by Christ, otherwise the risk, as laid out in Luke 11:26, is that the end may be worse than the beginning.

However, sometimes the occultic activity is historical, and this can leave a dark legacy, where the demonic claims ownership of a place. I will always remember blessing a house, with two others, where the occupants felt disturbed and anxious. We felt that we had done what God had called us to do. But a week later the couple came back to us and said that it was worse, and they felt awful. We went back again, but this time we went through the whole house, including the attic. It was in the attic that we found black candles, a makeshift altar, and signs of satanic worship. Having duly cleansed the house, including the attic, peace came to the owners. The moral of the story: if you bless a house, do not miss out any of the rooms, including the attic. Cleansing of a house is not a symbolic activity in the sense that you stand in one room and claim the house for God; it is the taking of ownership of a place for the presence of God.

Do not forget the land. I have come across at least three cases where buildings for one reason or another were built on ancient burial grounds. This can cause patterns of upset (very similar to churches being built on pagan sites) for those living in the houses. These can be varied, ranging from sickness to marriage break-ups, or just a sense of disturbance. In each case, we need to ask God for discernment and pray for the cleansing and blessing of the land itself. This stands within the theology of the cleansing of the land, which was the basis behind how the Israelites were to deal with those tribes they met upon entering the promised land.

Theologically, there are good grounds for cleansing the land, and it sits in the wider context of creation, where God wants to restore, or as Paul puts it in Romans:

> For the creation waits in eager expectation for the children of God to be revealed. For the creation was subjected to frustration, not by its own choice, but by the will of the one who subjected it, in hope that the creation itself will be liberated from its bondage to decay and brought into the freedom and glory of the children of God.
> *Romans 8:19-21*

As children of God we are called 'co-heirs with Christ' (Romans 8:17) and called to bring in that liberation. This is a ministry of the power of the cross, and the defeat of evil. Because it is such a ministry, we need to be careful of dilution. As we have seen, Jesus dealt with the demonic simply and directly. We move in that same authority and power. We bless, we cleanse, we release. This is not vague, because we do it in the authority of Christ.

Another aspect of the 'unquiet dead' is that they can be genuine human spirits. In 1995, David Lawrence published *Heaven: It's Not the End of the World*, and in this book he goes through all the biblical references to heaven and how life looks after death.[28] Tom Wright, a leading British New Testament scholar, endorsed this book as 'a clear and positive presentation'. David Lawrence draws the conclusion that after death we pass, if we are Christians, into paradise (Luke 23:43); if we are not Christians, into Hades. Hades is not hell, but the place which is the precursor to resurrection and judgement, after which there is hell. As Lawrence points out, the separation between the world as we know it now and the spiritual world is not absolute. (In Luke 16:19-31, the separation referred to between Lazarus and the rich man exists between Hades and paradise, not between the world and Hades.) In Hebrews 9:27 it says, 'man is destined to die once, and after that to face judgment' (NIV 1984), which agrees with Lawrence's analysis. We do all die once in this life and we will all face judgement; but this does not preclude the biblical Hades.

Spiritual beings like angels and demons are able to pass into this world. Given this situation, it is not beyond the realms of possibility that human spirits get stuck in trauma and can be experienced in this world. This would be about trying to resolve the hurt. Interestingly, this makes sense practically, as I have never come across a Christian human spirit, presumably because, who would need, or indeed want to, return from paradise? This can be a contentious issue theologically, not least because we are dealing with drawing together different strands of Scripture, and highlights the absolute necessity to discern what is happening by prayer in relationship with Christ.

---

[28] David Lawrence, *Heaven: It's Not the End of the World* (Milton Keynes: Scripture Union, 1995).

In psychological terms, people can get locked into an event or trauma that has taken place in the past and never get beyond that point. In general terms what locks someone into a past event is the relationship they have with the event (normally traumatic); it may cause feelings of guilt, anger or shame. They can never move on, the event never becomes history, and always lives in the present. Post-traumatic stress disorder is an example of this. In spiritual terms, it may be occasionally possible that human spirits can get locked in, for much the same reason, and the reason that they are being sensed is that they want to be released.

Where there is no evidence of occultic involvement, then the above option needs to be prayerfully considered. The best way I have found of bringing peace into a home where I believe a human spirit is present is to release them in the name of Christ into the hands of God.

This must not be confused, though, with the bereavement process, where it is quite normal for the bereaved to see or hear their loved one. In time this should diminish, as the bereaved process their loss. This can take a considerable time, and I would allow at least two years after the death of a loved one for these sensations to diminish.

Chapter 10
Staying Safe in the Deliverance Ministry as an Individual and as a Church

One of the most difficult things in the deliverance ministry is to see it as part of the normal Christian life. In the UK, we have lost touch with our Celtic Christian heritage and substituted a mixture of rationalism, individualism and unbelief. In the modern Celtic liturgies there is an emphasis on protection, and prayers that surround us with the love and presence of God. (These are called casting prayers.) Although it is an argued point as to whether modern Celtic liturgy has anything to do with the original Celtic Church, what is without a doubt true is that the Celtic Church was monastic, and well aware of the dangers it faced.

Normalisation is not the same as overemphasis. In some churches there is an overwhelming sense of the demonic that has resulted in some tragic abuse cases. This is almost the opposite polarity of the majority of the Western church. The danger here is that everything is the demonic.

One of the potential underlying problems in this area is fear. The idea of the demonic easily hits our fears at all sorts of levels, so it is much easier to avoid it if we can. Secondly, the demonic forces us into the realisation that we are in a battle. This does not make for comfortable Christianity. Thirdly, the demonic faces us with our weaknesses and a robust theology of sin. Fourthly, the demonic demands a response of holiness. Much easier all round not to engage!

However, society demands that Christianity delivers the goods; society is searching for spirituality. The authenticity of the Church has to be seen, the love of God has to be real. Perhaps this is in part the reason for the rise of the 'new monastic movement'. So to hold the balance, what is needed, firstly and above all else, is an ongoing and deepening relationship with Christ.

This must be a relationship, like all others, that is experienced and known; indeed, that is the role of the Holy Spirit. This has to be a relationship that is characterised by honesty and openness, based on love. But this is far from easy, partly because our relationship with Christ is determined at least initially to a large extent by our relationship experience of the past. We may want and crave a relationship of love with God. Our head knows that He is like this, but underneath all the time we are feeling and expecting the judgemental condemning weight of our experience of our human father or caregiver.

For Jesus, normality was defined by the relationship with His Father. It was here that He knew what He should be doing and when. So it should be for us, as from this relationship flows the capacity to discern what is demonic and what is not. Being in this relationship is what defines our capacity to trust and not to fear.

This extends to all walks of life. We tend to think of mindfulness as a recent phenomenon in the West, but being truly mindful is there in Matthew's Gospel:

> Therefore I tell you, do not worry about your life, what you will eat or drink; or about your body, what you will wear. Is not life more than food, and the body more than clothes? Look at the birds of the air; they do not sow or reap or store away in barns, and yet your heavenly Father feeds them. Are you not much more valuable than they? Can any one of you by worrying add a single hour to your life?
>
> And why do you worry about clothes? See how the flowers of the field grow. They do not labour or spin. Yet I tell you that not even Solomon in all his splendour was dressed like one of these. If that is how God clothes the grass of the field, which is here today and tomorrow is thrown into the fire, will he not much more clothe you—you of little faith? So do not worry, saying, 'What shall we eat?' or 'What shall we drink?' or 'What shall we wear?' For the pagans run after all these things, and your heavenly Father knows that you need them. But seek first his kingdom and his righteousness, and all these things will be given to you as well. Therefore do not worry about tomorrow, for tomorrow will worry about itself. Each day has enough trouble of its own.
> *Matthew 6:25-34*

Staying in the present, so as to genuinely engage with the Father, is critical to normalisation. It is in the present that I experience and know the presence of God. It is here that I know that I am surrounded with His love and protected. It is here that I know the promptings of the Spirit. What happens when I engage with Christ is that His normality becomes mine. For Jesus, the key was the mission, the kingdom of God; He came to bring in the kingdom. For us as individuals and the Church it is the same.

The role of the deliverance ministry here is clear, as we saw in Chapter 3. Nowhere else is the reality of the kingdom so clearly seen. But there is an element of the kingdom coming in, but not yet here in its fullness. We have wars, we have famines… it is clear that we are not yet in the fullness of the kingdom! But we are in the movement towards the kingdom. The deliverance ministry will call for increased holiness, facing our weaknesses and supporting one another. This is going to get messy and uncomfortable. Psalm 22 is an excellent example of how messy and mixed-up things can get, great hurt and pain being expressed to God, along with hope in the God who rescues.

My God, my God, why have you forsaken me?
Psalm 22:1

Yet you are enthroned as the Holy One.
Psalm 22:3

It is, though, very easy to get caught here in a morass of hurting people all demanding attention, and lose the context of what God is doing and asking of us. Church leaders need to keep a clear overall focus: the aim is to see the kingdom of God coming in. Wholeness is a function of this; keeping the focus relationally on the Father is critical. As individuals face their own agendas for healing, leaders can easily get caught in the 80/20 rule, where 80 per cent of our time is taken up by the 20 per cent who shout loudest. Constantly, we need to remind each other about bringing the kingdom in, irrespective of how much we are hurting. The balance between challenge and support has to be maintained, as it is very easy to lose momentum. What the Church has and proclaims over and above any therapy, is that we are in relationship with the living God, and this relationship has to be shared. Working with this, though, particularly for church leaders, needs an awareness of boundaries. Church leadership is notorious for having poor boundaries, for being on call 24/7, always available, etc. Coupled with poor boundaries is the issue of isolation. The leader, by virtue of being a leader, will be to a degree isolated within the community he or she serves as a leader. Because people look towards a leader, having numerous projections, it is very hard for the leader to establish supportive relationships within the community he/she serves. This can create substantial internal pressures, giving rise to mental health issues. The following have been identified: depression, anxiety, loss of libido and sexual interest, and somatisation (back pain, loss of voice, etc.).

For church leaders to avoid these problems, supervision is needed. Supervision looks at the overall state of who one is, psychologically, spiritually, relationally, using reflective practice. Supervision is normal practice in the therapy profession, but not with many ministers. Supervision is the fence on the cliff; therapy is what happens if you go over the cliff! Slowly this is changing in the Church, though, and the value of supervision is being recognised. As it stands, some denominations may have their own supervisory structure, but for many it is not mandatory, so ministers need to seek it out for themselves. The organisation in the UK for this is APSE (Association of Pastoral Supervisors and Educators).[29] Supervision is critical as it can highlight areas that need attention before they become pathological and damage occurs.

Taking breaks, developing friendships, having outside interests are all important. Understanding what it is that energises and what it is that drains energy helps keep the balance. For example, I know that for me one of the things that really energises is spending time in quiet with God, and I find modern Celtic spirituality really helpful here. What drains me is dealing with individuals who are constantly demanding at all times of day and night, as it sets up an internal conflict in myself, where part of me thinks I really should help, and the other part of me wants to tell them to get lost! And if I tell them to call at another time, I am easily consumed by anxiety. Should I have helped? Will they be OK?

For the individual church, there is a need to be aware of the dynamics of the deliverance ministry. None of us function as individuals in this area; we are all part of one body. So how do we stay safe as a church?

The priority of the church, as for the individual, must be to hear what God is saying. How God speaks to His people

---

[29] http://www.pastoralsupervision.org.uk (accessed 24th October 2016).

is varied: through leaders, through those with a prophetic ministry, through Scripture, etc. But we in our church have found it extremely important to have a place and time where anyone can come to hear what God is saying to the church.

Every Saturday morning, we meet to listen to God. This involves laying down what we have brought, our agendas, our week, our hurts and joys, and being prepared just to listen to what God is saying. Some hear through Scripture; some hear through 'words'; some see pictorially – it may be a picture for example of fire, representing blessing. There is the freedom to get it wrong, to learn from each other. It has been the heartbeat of the church. There has been many an occasion when we heard God saying 'deal with this curse in prayer, pray for this issue', and we have done so. In the week that followed we have often said, 'Well, it was a good thing we prayed for this.' God leads His church. The meeting is open to everyone.

Regular cleansing of the buildings is necessary. Our buildings get a lot of footfall, and sometimes it is important to pray around the building, as from time to time people have come in and cursed the building and church. Our buildings also see a lot of people who are upset and grieving, and this also needs God's love and grace. Those who pray around the buildings tend to be those who come on a Saturday. Cleansing a building always necessitates listening to God, so that we know what to pray.

A dedicated prayer chain[30] is important, particularly at those times when we sense that the church is coming under

---

[30] People who are linked for prayer, usually through phone.

sustained spiritual attack. As previously mentioned, this is often just before a satanic festival.

Key to maintaining the outward dynamic of the kingdom is worship, as it is in worship that we meet with the risen Christ. Different people find different kinds of worship helpful in this, but whatever the format of worship, it must facilitate the meeting with God. Sometimes this meeting is very straightforward. I will always remember talking to a friend who had suffered from severe depression, and him saying that for him, worship at that time was the Communion. Even if everything else was black and grey, because he could physically eat and drink the wine, he knew that God loved him. There was no emotional connection at all, but there was still a physical one. If worship is about meeting with the risen Lord, then there is going to be change. You cannot meet with the risen Christ and come away the same. It is very easy to lose the impact and expectation of worship, be that liturgy or worship songs, and go with it without engagement. We choose to engage, God will not force us. There is a huge privilege in meeting the risen Lord together as the body of Christ, but sometimes we have become so conditioned by consumerism that our attitude is more 'well, I will see what this does for me' and worship itself becomes idolatrous as the focus is now me.

How we approach our corporate relationship to Christ is important. Jesus' ministry was impacted by how people viewed Him. We are told: 'He could not do any miracles there, except lay his hands on a few people who were ill and heal them. He was amazed at their lack of faith' (Mark 6:5-6). If Jesus' ministry was impacted by their lack of faith, how much more so will our worship be impacted in the same way. With the deliverance ministry comes an increase in expectation and faith; here the worship needs to keep pace.

The worship dynamic has a second focus. As we meet with Christ, because we do it corporately, we meet with each other. But now we meet in the presence of the risen Lord, so how we view each other takes on the attributes of how Christ sees us. So, relationally, love flows from the cross in our worship and between each other. We want the best for each other, and for our community. The kingdom is coming in.

We are in for the long haul, and there is little doubt dealing with the powers of evil can be extremely tiring as we walk with Christ. But Paul was always clear about this, as he says in 2 Timothy: 'I have fought the good fight, I have finished the race, I have kept the faith' (2 Timothy 4:7).

So it is for us. As Paul says in Ephesians, we do this by '[putting] on the full armour of God, so that when the day of evil comes, you may be able to stand your ground, and after you have done everything, to stand' (Ephesians 6:13). In all of this we are sustained, empowered and equipped by the risen Lord. One of my favourite scriptures is in Isaiah:

> But those who hope in the LORD
> will renew their strength.
> They will soar on wings like eagles;
> they will run and not grow weary,
> they will walk and not be faint.
> *Isaiah 40:31*

Chapter 11
Setting Up the Deliverance Ministry in the Church

When setting up the deliverance ministry in a church, the key issue is leadership and authority.

This is because in the deliverance ministry of Jesus, ultimate authority is seen; the kingdom has come. Authority is very easily abused, and as Jesus' authority came from being within the Trinity, so for us the place of authority is within His body, the Church. Because this authority is within the Church, it operates under the leadership of the Church. This authority is given to every Christian. There is no special gift of getting rid of the demonic or evil, because it is part and parcel of being a Christian.

In Luke 9:1 authority is given to the Twelve to deal with evil spirits. In Luke 10:17 we have the same authority given to the 72. In the Mark version of the commissioning of the Twelve (Mark 6:7) we again have the same authority given. In Mark's account of the Great Commission, Jesus authorises the Eleven to 'drive out demons' (Mark 16:17) in His name. Even if this is a later addition, this was the common experience of the early Church. Indeed, in AD 251 the Church in Rome had 52 exorcists on its books, which was more than the number of presbyters![31] It is also noteworthy that this Commission in Mark takes place after Jesus' resurrection. There is still need to drive out demons, even though Satan has been defeated on the cross.

Jesus gave authority to deliver the demon-possessed to the Twelve, to the 72, and later this authority is given to the early Church. In the Acts of the Apostles we see this continuation of His ministry, not only in healing the sick, but also in the healing of those tormented by evil spirits, and we are told 'all of them were healed' (Acts 5:16).

With authority goes accountability. As we have noted, Jesus' authority and accountability was being part of the Trinity, and in Paul's analogy of the body, Christ is the head of the Church and we are accountable to Him (1 Corinthians 12:12-31).

Within the Church this is expressed by leadership. Within the Christian Church, leadership is not a function of power or of status, but of gifting. It is a gift given by the Holy Spirit: 'If a man's gift … is leadership, let him govern diligently' (Romans 12: 6-8, NIV 1984).

If we believe that God has called certain people to be leaders in a particular church, then we need to understand that ministering without their approval (and accountability to them) is, in effect, rebellion against God's leadership, and is therefore sin. This is not to advocate wholesale unthinking obedience, but to recognise that spiritual warfare cannot be undertaken without the authority of God recognised and affirmed by the leadership of the church.

---

[31] Chadwick, *The Early Church*, p.57.

This does have some difficult consequences at times. A few years ago I was talking to a couple after a conference, and they were saying, 'What do we do? Our minister does not believe in this area at all.' My answer was that under those circumstances they did not have the authority to carry out the deliverance ministry in that church. The options they then faced were to stay in the church and prayerfully ask God to change things, or to find another church. What would be categorically wrong would be to carry out the deliverance ministry without leadership approval, as this would potentially lead to splits and breaking of relationships. Also, and perhaps most critically, there would be an absence of pastoral care after the ministry. All of which would play into the hands of the demonic.

Sometimes people see this area as a specialised ministry. That is theologically wrong. We are *all* called, but it is true, as in most areas of church life, that some will have more experience than others, and we are always learning! One of the weaknesses in the Western Church has been to relegate this area to specialists.

Leadership in this area is also key. If authority is given in the context of the church, how deliverance ministry is then led is important. There are many books on leadership, but the deliverance ministry highlights certain aspects that we need to be aware of. One of which is the ability to hold a wider vision.

Because the deliverance ministry is still seen as something not mainstream or normal, it has the ability to cause fear and worry. Jesus always held His ministry in the context of the kingdom of God coming in. He held a bigger vision over and above what could be very dire circumstances. For example, in Gethsemane He could see and hold the wider picture. This is true of all the great leaders in the Bible; they could see that God was in control despite what was going on around them. One of the greatest examples of this is Moses. Time and time again he faces disaster: at the Red Sea; when the Israelites are running out of water and food; when they actually come to the Promised Land, and are scared off by the spies' report (except Caleb and Joshua). In the deliverance ministry we are solely dependent on the authority of God, and at times we have to trust despite what is going on around us. In our church life this has been most obvious at our 'listening' prayer meeting. Many times God has simply said, 'Trust and obey.' Part of holding the vision is discernment, which we looked at in Chapter 4; but for the leader there is another element – the ability to see patterns. One person ill is one person; ten people ill who are all key leaders is something else. Often it is only the leader who has the overall information. The leader is often the one who has to discern prophecy. In our church, the prophetic ministry is held predominantly within the 'listening' prayer meeting, where we have those who are gifted with prophecy. The leader needs to know who to listen to. This is not as straightforward as it seems, as in my experience, prophecy is very rarely 100 per cent of God, but much more like 50 per cent God, 50 per cent the individual.

To lead takes courage and faith, which is not a function of trying to make myself secure, by repeating Scripture as a mantra, but much more about acknowledging my weaknesses before God and allowing Him to minister to me, in my fears, in my failings. To lead is going to hurt. Jesus wept on occasion (see John 11:35; Luke 19:41). You cannot genuinely lead without the ability to hear and pick up the pain of others. You have to know how to put it down, but you also have to be prepared to walk alongside.

If vision is the first prerequisite, the second is humility. I cannot do this by myself; even Jesus gathered from within the Twelve three who particularly supported Him. Moses needed two to support his arms in the battle with the Amalekites (Exodus 17:12). Leadership needs humility to recognise our dependence on one another, and that includes me. Part of humility is the ability to know I get it wrong, and recognise and deal with my weaknesses. This has a very practical element to it, in that as a leader I need a place to go where I can be honest, look at myself, and get whatever extra support is needed (as previously mentioned, supervision is good for this).

Wear authority with compassion. In this area it is very easy to be absolute, not to listen carefully. Yes, I am going to have to take decisions, but all the time I am dealing with people whom God loves and wants to bring to healing and wholeness. Do not be hurried by demands, which in all probability are a reflection of the fear of others. Take time to listen; Jesus did. He went into the hills (Mark 6:46).

Who should be involved?

The short answer is that everybody is involved, but some are going to be more involved than others! Churches that are growing, sharing the gospel, moving out into the community, are all going to be subject to attack. So who is going to deal with it?

It is unfortunate that this area can be a source of fascination for some. These are the ones who cannot hold the balance or context of the deliverance ministry. For them it is exciting, thrilling, and gives them a kick. They do not want it to be part of the normal Christian life; they want to feel special because they are involved in it. All of which is rooted in their own personality. Often this is expressed in 'feeling called to this area'. I am very wary of those who feel this! This is not to say that they are wrong, but there may well be a personal agenda they are not facing up to. On the whole, and in an ideal world, you are looking for those who have a great deal of common sense, and are well-grounded. They may well be the ones you have to ask to be involved. This is not a specialised area, so those who are involved in the healing ministry should automatically be included, as should church leadership. This may well require a great deal of teaching.[32] It is always best to start small and build up gradually!

For those involved in this ministry, certain gifts are necessary and may well be already present:

Discernment
1 Corinthians 12:10: 'to another the ability to distinguish between spirits' (ESV). This is the key gift for anyone who is involved in this ministry. This is what you have to have. However, like all the gifts, this is not a given in the sense of a present to own, but a gift that is relationally based in Christ.

---

[32] See www.restoring-the-apple.org (accessed 24th October 2016).

Wisdom

'If any of you lacks wisdom, you should ask God, who gives generously to all without finding fault, and it will be given to you' (James 1:5). (This is not to be confused with the 'message of wisdom' in 1 Corinthians 12:8.) Wisdom given by God allows us to see an overall picture. This is particularly important in the deliverance ministry, as there are always psychological factors involved, and these need to be recognised. If in doubt, take time!

Holiness

> Rather, join with me in suffering for the gospel,
> by the power of God. He has saved us and called
> us to a holy life – not because of anything we have
> done but because of his own purpose and grace.
> This grace was given us in Christ Jesus before the
> beginning of time.
> *2 Timothy 1:8b-9*

Holiness is not being pious; holiness is not doing; holiness is living in relationship with Christ and seeing all things as subject to that relationship. It does not mean perfection, or a smooth ride; it does mean vulnerability, and knowing you can get it wrong. Holiness is being real and human with God and others, because I know I am accepted and loved without condition by God. Holiness is growing in love.

Along with these gifts goes the issue of authority. It is simply no good having people in this area who have serious issues with authority. These issues must be addressed first.

Practicalities

For each church the practicalities of this ministry are going to be different, but our experience may be helpful.

Firstly, teaching that is open to the whole church. We have specifically developed a teaching course which you can download at http://www.restoring-the-apple.org. This course includes six video sessions and a handbook. This book is designed to go alongside the course.

Secondly, we found that of key importance is our listening prayer meeting. It is here that the sensitivity to hear God is developed and tested.

Thirdly, we have a prayer chain that deals entirely with this area. Those involved in the chain do have the gifts talked about earlier in the chapter. This chain is not large (it comprises ten people) and is only activated by the leadership of the church. In the main, the chain deals with demonic attack on the church in the widest sense. It will not deal with individuals.

Fourthly, we have a core of about 15 people who are used in such areas as praying for houses and individuals, prayer-walking, and cleansing the church buildings.

Problems we have faced

By far the biggest issues that we have faced have been relational. Because the demonic wants to destroy our relationship with God and with each other, this is the area that is most often targeted. This, coupled with the fact that we are all wounded to a greater or lesser degree, means issues are always arising. This is not new! Paul had to continually tackle these issues in Corinth and no doubt in his other churches as well. How we deal with this is one of the great challenges of the wider Church, and is a matter for ongoing exploration. It is very easy to get all-consumed and deflected by the personal issues that arise; maintaining the balance of healing in the context of the outward movement of the kingdom requires continual monitoring.

Looking ahead

In an age where the Western world is dominated by the idolatry of individualism, Christian identity becomes more and more critical. Individualism easily leads to relativism – what you believe is your business and has nothing to do with me. This does not sit easily with the good news that Jesus came to bring, which He saw as relevant and necessary for the whole of humankind. What is equally worrying is that individualism does not work very well in relationships, and that has a massive impact on the witness of the Church: 'By this everyone will know that you are my disciples, if you love one another' (John 13:35). In working this out we are coming head to head with Paul's 'powers of this dark world and against the spiritual forces of evil in the heavenly realms' (Ephesians 6:12). For Jesus, this involved taking on evil in all its forms, and so it should for us. A major component part of this for Jesus was the deliverance ministry. This cannot be avoided by the Church any longer.

Our identity as children of the living God compels us to walk as Jesus walked. This sits very uncomfortably with our Western Enlightment mindset. This is not a bad thing, providing it does not lead to the polarities of disbelief on the one hand and 'everything is demonic' on the other. The tension should lead us with humility to continually seek to know what God is saying here, and relationally with Christ, bring the kingdom of God in.

To God be the glory.

Amen.